Same God
Different
Churches

A Guide to Christian Denominations

Same God
Different
Churches

A Guide to Christian Denominations

BY KATIE MEIER

TRANSIT®

www.TransitBooks.com
A Division of Thomas Nelson, Inc.
www.ThomasNelson.com

SAME GOD, DIFFERENT CHURCHES:
A GUIDE TO CHRISTIAN DENOMINATIONS

Published in Nashville, Tennessee, by Tommy Nelson®, a Division of Thomas Nelson, Inc. Visit us on the Web at www.tommynelson.com.

Tommy Nelson® books may be purchased in bulk for educational, business, fund-raising, or sales promotional use. For information, please email SpecialMarkets@ThomasNelson.com.

Unless otherwise marked, Scripture quotations in this book are from the King James Version of the Holy Bible (KJV).

Scripture marked (NCV) is quoted from *The Holy Bible, New Century Version*®, copyright © 1987, 1988, 1991 by Word Publishing, a division of Thomas Nelson, Inc. Used by permission.

Library of Congress Cataloging-in-Publication Data
Meier, Katie.
Same God, different churches: a guide to Christian denominations / by Katie Meier.
     p. cm.
Includes index.
ISBN 1-4003-0547-0 (softcover)
1. Christian sects. I. Title.
BR157.M45 2005
280—dc22

2005006393

Printed in China

05 06 07 08 09 — 5 4 3 2 1

CAN'T FIND YOUR CHURCH IN THIS BOOK?

Although this book takes a look at some of the longest-standing Christian groups in American history and provides a basic lineup of churches to learn about, the space limitations within these pages make it impossible to provide a listing of every Christian church group or denomination in the USA. So be aware that Christianity comes in a wealth of other forms not covered here. And remember that churches with similar names can have very different approaches to Christian worship.

Also, churches can establish, merge, regroup, or redefine themselves. So keep in mind that the information in this book, though current at press time, might also change. Before visiting a church for the first time, it's a good idea to call and speak to a pastor, go online, or write to request church materials be sent so you can have the most current info available.

URL LINK NOT WORKING?

The Web links throughout this book are the quickest way to get info on the churches profiled, but don't forget: The Web's a living thing. Websites change, get deleted, and information can be moved from one place to another as churches reorganize and update their websites. So while the links were all verified and current when *Same God, Different Churches* went to print, some links might not work later.

CONTENTS

Have you ever wondered why there are so many kinds of Christians? Why people have so many titles, names, and descriptions for the styles of Christianity they practice, even though they all look to the same God? Someone might say, "Yeah, I'm a Christian. I go to church over at Southside Bible." Or you hear someone say, "I'm Episcopalian," or "I go to an Assemblies of God Church."

All the labels Christians use to describe their specific styles of worship or belief can be more confusing than helpful. It can be hard to tell one group from another, or figure out what each kind of Christian church teaches just by hearing the name. In fact, lots of us know we're believers but aren't quite sure what specifically makes us a Lutheran, Catholic, or an Emergent Christian.

Here's the truth, though: Christianity will work in your life only if you know what's up with what you believe. Each kind of Christianity tells the story of God's truth in a different way. And it's this story that provides a kind of map for the specific kind of Christian life you'll live. The way you read the Bible, the priorities that get your attention, and the opinions you hold about politics, the environment, or social issues have everything to do with the kind of Christianity you're hooked up with.

In this book you'll get to the bottom of Christian labels as you're brought up to speed on the back story that shapes the way your church rolls, what people there emphasize, and how it's different from other Christian groups.

What's the kind of Christianity you practice all about?

In Part One you'll find information and quizzes to get you thinking about your own beliefs, and to help you understand those of friends and family whose beliefs are different. Then in Part Two of the book, your quiz answers from Part One will lead you to a set of church profiles. These profiles have been divided into four color groups:

ROSE (A): EVANGELICAL and CONSERVATIVE

If you come up with a lot of ROSE (A) answers on the quizzes, you're probably an evangelical/conservative kind of Christian. The labels "evangelical" and "conservative" cover churches where people look to the Bible as the most direct source of info for Christian living and encourage people to get out there, share their faith, and bring others to Christ. You'll find some flexibility in the ways people interpret God's Word at churches in the evangelical/conservative group. For example, not all churches in this group teach that the Bible should be read literally. But no matter which church you check out from this list, you'll find conservative Christians who consider the Bible God's inspired Word, who focus on salvation and a personal relationship with Jesus and on spreading the Gospel message through evangelism.

TEAL (B): TRADITIONAL

If you come up with a lot of TEAL (B) answers on the quizzes, you're probably a traditional kind of Christian. "Traditional" is the label used for churches where ancient Christian traditions and the church fathers define worship styles, biblical interpretation, leadership roles, and ways people connect with God. Churches in this group have deep histories and want people to mine the past so they can draw upon examples of Christians who've lived particularly holy lives, respecting them as saints. Traditional churches are biblical, centered on Christian living, and encourage people to be in relationship with God, often through the use of rituals instead of things like born-again experiences or the giving of testimony. And it's in these rituals that traditional churches preserve Christian history. From worship styles to the words recited at every service, it's all symbolic, it's all got a specific purpose, and it's all been done like that for years.

BLUE (C): ECSTATIC

If you come up with a lot of **BLUE (C)** answers on the quizzes, you're probably an ecstatic kind of Christian. "Ecstatic" is the label used for churches where believers are encouraged to display the emotions, feelings, and gifts brought on by the Holy Spirit. The role of the Holy Spirit—sometimes called the Holy Ghost at churches in this group—is central to ecstatic worship and plays a huge part in the development of spiritual maturity for each believer. Worship services at ecstatic churches are high-energy, as people support one another in going with the flow, dancing, singing, or getting into praise with their whole bodies as they feel moved by the Spirit as a way to connect with God. The Bible is front and center in terms of guiding the lives of believers at ecstatic churches. Biblical interpretations and beliefs are conservative, and God's Word is the final deal for every facet of life.

PURPLE (D): MAINLINE and MODERATE

If you come up with a lot of **PURPLE (D)** answers on the quizzes, you're probably a mainline/moderate kind of Christian. "Mainline" is a label used to describe churches that have histories on the American scene, making them well established as opposed to, say, a new church that just began a few years ago. The history of each mainline or moderate church makes it unique, since each developed over time to serve specific needs, to encourage people to live specific kinds of lifestyles, or to worship in specific kinds of ways. That means churches in this group might range from conservative to moderate in terms of biblical interpretation, have distinctive social causes members put at the forefront of their faith, be full of members who've adopted particular lifestyles, or who worship in a way that clicks with one particular kind of ethnic, cultural, or racial group.

As you read through the book, these profiles should help you sharpen the focus of your own faith. Better than that, though, the book can work as a way for you to understand Christianity on a whole other level. Well, on a bunch of other levels, actually, since the book makes plain what different kinds of Christians have in common (Christ), where they differ (certain biblical interpretations), and what bonds us all somewhere in the middle (the desire to connect with God). So read on and have at it. Make Christianity real by making it your own.

Are you open to learning more about your faith?

PART 1

Same God

Same God, Different Christians

How Things Got that Way

Christians all believe in Jesus. We all believe He died, rose again, and gave us new life. But did you know:

- Christians don't all have the same books in their Bibles?
- Some Christians believe the Holy Spirit allows them to speak a foreign, spiritual language?
- Women lead some churches, but aren't allowed to be in leadership positions in other churches?

So while Christianity *can be* defined by a belief in salvation as Jesus offers it, it *can't be* defined by the way people worship God in thanks for this gift.

Christianity is all over the place when it comes to which parts of faith Christians choose to focus on, the ways they want to live out their beliefs, and the ways they choose to set up their churches. This guarantees Christians will be Christians no matter which church we attend, but that each type of Christianity will be a little bit different.

The differences in Christian theology developed over time. Some people thought the story of God's truth should be told one way. Other people wanted it told another way. So theology has changed with each new generation of Christians. (Theology is basically the how-it-all-works instructional-info stuff related to God—writings that sum up the way things work.) First, God created the heavens and the earth, then stories of creation, life, and God's will got written down; finally, theologians got together, read these stories, debated a bunch of different points, agreed on some things, didn't agree on others, decided to each start their own kind of Christian church, and lots of years later you ended up in one of them. Done deal.

Ah, but not so quick. It'd be cool if Christian history could be summed up in a paragraph, but we need more info. Let's start with the apostles. In a time when believing in a single God wasn't that cool, the apostles made the scene with their modified Jewish beliefs. God's message as revealed and preached by Jesus claimed it could take the worst of people and make them new. Jesus was crucified and rose again to show people the kind of transformation He was talking about.

After the death of Jesus the apostles spread this message, leading others to become believers and start creating church communities. But if you've read the New Testament letters of the apostle Paul, you know that not everybody thought alike. People didn't always agree on the ways God's message should be interpreted, or followed, or taught. From day one, Christians had different ideas about how to live for Jesus and what to make of His message.

Has your church ever had a big disagreement?

3

So as time passed churches grew, and leaders of the Christian faith began to emerge in different places, from Africa to Europe. A few of these leaders agreed it was time to gather up everything that had been written about Jesus. Eventually, these collections were trimmed down and combined into what we know today as the Bible. But before that happened, these leaders first went to a bunch of meetings. Each time church leaders met, they prayed for God's guidance, and eventually ended up agreeing on which writings were the real deal and which were too sketchy to trust.

But the meetings were a lot like working on a group project for school; there were lots of opinions. Some Christians at the meetings were know-it-alls, others were peacemakers, and, of course, you know there's gotta be the control freak, right? And then you had the "I refuse to make a choice until God shows me a miracle" guy and the huffy-puffy "I never get my way" guy and the classic "You can do what you want . . . but I'm obviously right" guy. Every kind of personality type worked together to make decisions about which writings would become Scripture and which wouldn't. God led the process, but church leaders also had to use what they knew about Christian truth to vote out some of the writings. After about four big-time meetings, what we know as the New Testament was finalized.

God led the process.

4

Following are the main points:

- People who lived when Jesus lived didn't have a Bible. They believed in His message based on what they saw and heard.
- Lots of people wrote down what they saw and believed.
- All that writing created a huge paper trail.
- Church leaders had meetings about this paper trail, which led to debates and prayer.
- God guided the process of narrowing things down to the writings we know as the New Testament.

With the New Testament (NT) done, it was time to focus on the Hebrew writings. These had already been compiled by Jewish leaders two centuries before the birth of Christ, so our Christian Old Testament (OT) is a collection of Hebrew writings about the God whom Jews know as Elohim, El Shaddai, Adonai, or Ha-Shem (The Name).

Because Jesus came after the time of the Hebrew writings and delivered a new message, Christians use the word *old* for the Hebrew writings in our Bible. But the old/new thing is specifically Christian. Jews don't call their writings *old*. After all, since most Jews don't believe Jesus was the Messiah, they don't have a new message that would make their original writings old.

Jews call their writings the Hebrew Scriptures, or the Tanakh (ta-noth).

Where it gets interesting is when it comes to which Hebrew Scriptures Christians decided God was leading them to use in the Old Testament. This is where we get our first glimpse of Christian beliefs going off in different directions, even though all eyes are still focused on Jesus. Though you might think God could just show people which Scriptures to pick, when church leaders followed God's advice, they felt led in different directions. The solution to this dilemma was to come up with a formula—or a set of standards for judging which Hebrew Scriptures to keep. If a Scripture lived up to the standards, it stayed. If not, it was bye-bye time. The writings were not included.

Or was it? When OT cuts had to be made, Christians split on their opinions rather than lose writings they felt led by God to keep. Nobody had any problem keeping all the books already included in the Hebrew Scriptures. But people did have a problem when it came to other books being used in various Jewish and Christian circles. These books weren't officially included in Jewish Scriptures, but the books did tell stories of Jewish history and featured people living inspirational lives of faith; and they were used in a casual kind of way in different communities of faith for instruction, inspiration, or education. So when it came time to put together the Christian OT, some Christian leaders felt the books were close enough to the standards to be included; other Christian leaders disagreed.

In the end, Orthodox and Catholic Christians both included some of the extra books in their versions of the OT; Protestant Christians didn't. That's why today you've got Orthodox Bibles with forty-nine books of OT Scripture, Catholic Bibles with forty-six books, and Protestant Bibles with just thirty-nine books in the OT. The extra books included in the Orthodox and Catholic Bibles are usually called the *Apocrypha* (uh-pock-rah-fa). This word started out in Greek meaning "hidden," but later it was translated into Latin and then into Middle English where the word came to mean "not authentic."

"So who's right?" you're asking. "Isn't there just one truth when it comes to God?" I'm not gonna try to smooth things over or make it seem like everything's all good when it comes to Christian groups agreeing with all the others. Truth is, they don't. A lot of Christians are suspicious of one another. They think that the others have messed up God's message or that they've taken Scripture way out of context. All that's really gone on, though, is that each kind of Christian (Orthodox, Catholic, and Protestant) has stayed true to the set of OT writings they think best tells the story of God's truth. Check out the following table to see which books made the OT cut for each group of believers.

THE OLD TESTAMENT [OT]

Orthodox	Catholic	Protestant
Genesis	Genesis	Genesis
Exodus	Exodus	Exodus
Leviticus	Leviticus	Leviticus
Numbers	Numbers	Numbers
Deuteronomy	Deuteronomy	Deuteronomy
Joshua	Joshua	Joshua
Judges	Judges	Judges
Ruth	Ruth	Ruth
1 Samuel	1 Samuel	1 Samuel
2 Samuel	2 Samuel	2 Samuel
1 Kings	1 Kings	1 Kings
2 Kings	2 Kings	2 Kings
1 Chronicles	1 Chronicles	1 Chronicles
2 Chronicles	2 Chronicles	2 Chronicles
1 Esdras		
Ezra	Ezra	Ezra
Nehemiah	Nehemiah	Nehemiah
Tobit	Tobit	
Judith	Judith	
Esther	Esther	Esther
Maccabees 1	Maccabees 1	
Maccabees 2	Maccabees 2	
Maccabees 3		
Job	Job	Job

Orthodox	Catholic	Protestant
Psalms (151)	Psalms	Psalms
Prayer of Manasseh		
Proverbs	Proverbs	Proverbs
Ecclesiastes	Ecclesiastes	Ecclesiastes
Song of Solomon	Song of Solomon	Song of Solomon
Wisdom of Solomon	Wisdom of Solomon	
Sirach	Sirach	
Isaiah	Isaiah	Isaiah
Jeremiah	Jeremiah	Jeremiah
Lamentations	Lamentations	Lamentations
Baruch	Baruch	
Ezekiel	Ezekiel	Ezekiel
Daniel	Daniel	Daniel
Hosea	Hosea	Hosea
Joel	Joel	Joel
Amos	Amos	Amos
Obadiah	Obadiah	Obadiah
Jonah	Jonah	Jonah
Micah	Micah	Micah
Nahum	Nahum	Nahum
Habakkuk	Habakkuk	Habakkuk
Zephaniah	Zephaniah	Zephaniah
Haggai	Haggai	Haggai
Zechariah	Zechariah	Zechariah
Malachi	Malachi	Malachi

See some blanks here and there in the list of Bible books? Those are the places where some kinds of Christians took one route and some took another. And if you've never heard of some of the books on these lists, you're not alone. I won't name names (. . . ahem, me), but I once heard a story about a Protestant girl who went mental after looking through her mom's Roman Catholic Bible.

"Surely there must be a HUGE mistake," she said. "Wisdom of Solomon?! Who put that in there?" Then the unnamed girl proceeded to totally flip out.

The deal was, this girl wasn't as educated as she could have been about the bigger Christian picture. It's not that she needed to understand Christianity on a high theology level or anything, but learning that not all kinds of Christianity, or all kinds of Bibles, or even all kinds of Christians are the same would have been a solid first step toward spiritual maturity.

But it might have helped her to know why some Christians took one route and some took another. Some of the reasons:

- A set of standards helped church leaders decide which writings would make the cut to become the OT.
- Church leaders felt strongly that God was leading them; so strongly they didn't want to compromise, even though they were heading in

different directions. People didn't agree which writings met the standards and which didn't.

- Christian groups split the difference, each choosing an OT a little bit different from the others but still focusing their core belief in Christ and the message of the Gospels.

Of course, even now there's static over whose Bible translation is correct. Christians have been battling over Bible translations since . . . well, since the Bible came together as the official book of Christianity. Currently, Bibles are published that paraphrase, or restate, the words of the text, like *The New King James Version,* and there are also Bibles like *The Message* that use more of a slang approach, so at this point the words of the Bible are written differently and sound differently from Bible to Bible. You have to understand, though, it's not like Protestants ended up with a Bible that's got nine books in the whole thing while Orthodox Christians use a Bible that's got fifty-nine. That's not how it is at all. It's more like a percentage deal. Catholic Bibles (like the New American Bible) have about 15 percent more Scripture than Bibles Protestants read (like the New International Version). Then Orthodox Christians use Bible translations that have about 25 percent more Scripture than Protestants.

Do you have someone you can talk to about your religious questions?

Christian history is a history of difference. People have prayed for God's guidance but sometimes heard different things. This doesn't mean their commitment to following God's truth has been compromised, only that you shouldn't be surprised to find Christians hold some beliefs that are the same while others are different. So as long as you know a Christian group is dedicated to Christ and to following the gospel message in service of God's will, don't worry that other kinds of Christianity do things differently. Instead, listen to where God is leading you personally, and then decide how you believe the story of His truth should be told.

The debate over certain kinds of Christianity being right or wrong has been going on since the time of the apostles. Remember all the letters Paul sent to smooth out differences between different churches? The debate goes back that far and is now just another part of Christian life. The debate is renewed every time church sermons include negative or insulting things about another kind of Christianity, and spreads wider and wider every time Christians use this kind of info to gossip about the things another set of Christians believe.

The fact is, nobody knows the exact way God wants us to interpret the Bible or to live as Christians. The best anyone can do is to get into prayer with Him, read His Word, and pray for guidance because, you know what? No matter how much we think our beliefs are the exact right thing God intended all Christians to believe and do, our read of God's Word isn't perfect and neither are our lives. We fall into sin and don't always think clearly or act as maturely as we should. And at the end of the day we're not God's equals. We're His children, so we're never gonna know exactly what He's thinking or why He leads Christians to different beliefs. However, Christian communities are places we can draw strength, find mentors, and establish a solid lead on ways to live out our faith. Hooking up with a church that supports your growing knowledge of God is a good thing.

If you realize Christianity has got debates and rifts, you've taken the first step. But it won't protect you from hearing bad things about other Christians every so often. Just don't get sucked into this negativity, even if the trashing is based on a heartfelt belief that God is leading in a particular direction.

WHAT BELIEFS ARE STANDARD IN YOUR LIFE?

This quiz will help you figure out your standards of biblical interpretation and belief.

Church leaders used a set of standards to help determine which writings would make up the Bible. You can use a similar set of standards to figure out which church, or kind of Christianity, you practice.

Answer all the questions below based on the beliefs you think tell God's story best. When you're all done, check out what they mean at the end of the quiz.

1. **When people in your church or family talk about the Bible, they mostly focus on the fact that it's . . .**

A Inspired by God, totally true, and totally trustworthy.

B A sacred book of stories and teachings written under the inspiration of God.

C Error-free and is the final word when it comes to the way Christians should behave.

D Inspired by God, doesn't have to be read literally, but is the main source of examples, ideas, and stories about Christian life and virtue.

2. What's the church for?

A It's for following and celebrating Jesus and for spreading the gospel message.

B It's for passing down Christian traditions and the historical teachings of the apostles.

C It's the body of Christ and gets its life from the Holy Spirit so believers can receive spiritual blessings.

D It's for unity, fellowship, and connection with other Christians.

3. What kind of Scripture does your church focus on most?

A Paul's letters, some of the stories in the Gospels about Jesus and His followers, and main stuff from the Old Testament, like the Exodus story.

B We read through the Old and New Testaments on a schedule that spans one year, so we don't really focus on just one part of the Bible.

C We read a lot of stuff from Acts and from the Gospels. Not too much Old Testament, but some.

D Passages from the Old and New Testaments are read together during worship so we always get a mix of both.

4. How do people in your church celebrate, show God respect, or worship?

A People pray a lot, and there's usually singing, a choir, a band, or something like that. We also do Communion with grape juice and bread.

B People light candles, say prayers, chant, or sing; and we have lots of rituals, like the Eucharist.

C People sing, dance, and sometimes speak in tongues. The Lord's Supper is also celebrated, but not that often.

D Rituals are pretty common, like Communion. Sometimes we also try things like silent prayer, meditation, or get into something creative like art or dance.

5. What are sermons mostly about when you go to church?

A General Christianity stuff, like what the Bible says it means to be saved, justified, or called to spread the Gospel.

B Sermons are thematic, based on whatever Bible reading we had that day.

C Overcoming things that keep us down, like sin or Satan. A lot of sermons are about making sure we choose right over wrong, and are based on specific verses of Scripture.

D Sermons are tied in to current events or social issues a lot of times and reflect the overall sense of the Bible passages we're reading.

ANSWERS

If you picked mostly **A** answers, your faith is with Christians who like to focus on individual verses in the Gospels and break down what's going on as a model for living. A one-to-one type friendship with Jesus is something you're comfortable with, as the stories of His life and the words of His teachings are things you can relate to.

If you picked mostly **B** answers, your faith is with Christians who like to draw on traditions of the past as a way to connect with God in the present. The order and organization of faith is a kind of prayer, and themes of God's Word are used to draw out what's essential in Christian character and Christian living.

If you picked mostly **C** answers, your faith is with Christians who focus on the Holy Spirit and the spiritual gifts Christians can tap into as they mature in their faith. Full spiritual maturity is a gradual process but can be achieved, and it's cool to show or be open about the emotions and feelings this process brings on.

If you picked mostly **D** answers, your faith is with Christians who like to mix old and new together as a way to preserve Christian traditions but also make it easy for groups of Christians to grow toward God together. Biblical themes are tied together with a respect for the kind of life Jesus led and the power of this example for every generation.

Where Belief Comes From

Christian beliefs are a collection of truths; unfortunately, that truth doesn't just land in our lap and say, "Yo, what's up?!" Truth is something we have to find and decide to believe. For Christians, the search for truth starts with the Bible. Believers read and interpret Scripture, make decisions about big Christian truths like the divinity of Jesus or the reality of the Resurrection, and then make decisions about the smaller beliefs after that. For example, we might first come to believe Jesus is the Christ, or our Messiah, and decide what we believe about the kind of person Jesus was on earth, what His ministry meant, and what the main point of His message is for us today. After that, the other, smaller beliefs we'd decide on would include stuff like how we think the world was created, how the Holy Spirit comes into our lives, where we go after we die, or how God works in the lives of His people.

Our beliefs and perspectives about all these topics usually get passed along to us by people in our church. These people could be our parents, relatives, friends, mentors, or pastors. But the basic deal is that the church we start in and the people we know there play a huge role in what kind of Christians we become.

Have you made your faith your own?

Most of us get our primary info about what to believe and what makes God's Word true from listening to sermons, lectures, classes, retreats, or conferences. We rely on teachers, parents, mentors, or pastors to have and to provide us the right info. We take for granted that the people we listen to know what they're talking about; and we trust that they understand how a belief works—or is true—on a theological level. As we pick up their explanations and ideas, our faith becomes a kind of group-project deal.

Although absorbing the explanations and ideas of others is a solid way to develop your faith and learn the basics when you're younger, as you mature it's good to see the flip side: *If we're Christians who rely solely on borrowed beliefs, our spiritual growth can get stuck on pause.*

To grow, we must get down to the how-it-all-works kind of info that explains our beliefs so we can own our faith and really understand what we're living for. For example, the hard work behind the belief "God made us in His image" would require us to learn where God came from, why He created us, what it means that we're a reflection of Him, and a list of other things. The big beliefs state what's true. The hard work behind these beliefs makes the truth make sense on a logical level.

By doing the hard work, you will unlock the how-it-all-works theology behind your faith, making you the official owner of what you believe. This kind of knowledge makes Christianity really personal because it kicks down standard answers and lets you walk into a kind of spiritual confidence that's seriously powerful. So the reward is well worth it, but I won't kid you—learning how to own your own belief isn't an easy process. Check out the story of Cam to sum up how important it is, but how hard it can be, to own your beliefs.

CAM

In the big wide world lived a Christian named Cam—just your average Christian with a heart for God. As a little kid, Cam listened to JC the Jesus puppet tell stories in Sunday school. As a junior high kid, Cam played Ancient Hebrew #4 in the Christmas play each year. As a high-school kid, Cam learned the chords to "Come, Now Is the Time to Worship" and hung with the worship band. And along the way Cam went to college too. Not Christian college, though. Cam did the public college thing.

Cam had long heard secular colleges trashed for being places where good Christians go wrong or get into shady stuff, but public college didn't lack religion at all. Religion was everywhere, if Cam took the right classes. Almost every major had a few classes not just about religion, but about how the world works, why people are the way they are, how the universe was created, or how writing, art, music, or cultures throughout the world have a touch of the divine right down at the core.

Cam found this out by taking a class about literature. Things got heated when the class began to debate whether or not the Bible was just a regular book. And before he knew it, Cam was all up in people's faces going head to head with doubters.

But no matter how many times Cam thought people were just stirring stuff up as a way to seem liberal, progressive, or too smart to be religious, little bits of doubt kept popping up. Faith in the Bible was central to Cam's life, but why? How had Cam come to believe in Christianity, after all? And more importantly, why was it real? Why was it true?

Cam's doubt turned into frustration over these questions. Pretty quickly it became obvious that there was no explaining why—in Cam's own words—Christianity was real, true, or important. Cam had a solid set of beliefs based on the Bible, but didn't know exactly how the beliefs all worked. It was more like there was a standard answer and explanation for most questions Cam was asked about Christianity, but that was it. If pushed further, Cam had nothing in terms of the how-it-all-works theology behind the belief.

Let's say Cam was asked something like, "Well, how do you know you're saved?" No

How did you come to believe in Christianity?

big deal. Cam could handle it with a standard explanation, saying, "I know I'm saved because I've given my life to Jesus." But that is where it ended. And when Cam started to think about it on a deeper level, the end of it was the very start of the problem: Cam's standard explanation didn't actually answer the question being asked. The people bugging Cam were asking *how*. They wanted to know *how* salvation worked in terms of the nuts and bolts of it all. They wanted Cam to explain the things in Christianity that proved salvation was real and worked as Christians said it did.

Cam's class went from debates about the Bible to talking about specific Bible stories and the things going on in them. At that point the class debates got hotter than ever since Bible stories about miracles, the Resurrection, and the end times were thrown out to everybody in class for discussion. Faced with challenges to Christianity from the doubters in the class, Cam went the church route first, trying to come up with solid answers. There had to be a sermon or Bible study or article or book or something to rely on. Then it hit Cam: borrowed beliefs! Cam was using borrowed beliefs and had no idea how to do the biblical interpreting and explaining behind Christian belief.

As luck would have it, though, a few other Christians were in Cam's class and seemed

Cam was using borrowed beliefs.

to be in the same boat. Well, it turned out to be more like there were three boats: Cam's boat and two others—one on each side of Cam.

The boat to the right of Cam was full of believers, but they weren't believers who'd realized they'd been borrowing their beliefs. (For the sake of discussion, we'll call this boat the Christians.) These believers were still trying to pull out explanations and interpretations they'd heard at church as a way to defend their faith.

The boat to the left was full of Christians who knew they'd been borrowing their beliefs; however, instead of learning more about their faith, they had decided to dump it all together, making them technically a boat of ex-Christians. The people in this boat got all philosophical about everything in class, saying they were done with Christianity because how could anyone prove the existence of a divine Being like God, much less disprove the idea that people didn't crawl up out of the primordial ooze and evolve into what you see today.

So during all the class debates, things were tense among the boats since two were full of people so frustrated by the others they couldn't wait to lay down the hammer, proving their point once and for all.

In the boat to the left of Cam with the philosophical crew, one girl became the main spokesperson. We'll call her Captain TTL (Captain to the left of Cam). Sick of hearing the same standard beliefs she'd been raised on used as a defense by the Christians, Captain TTL went off listing all the standard answers Christians usually give to most questions—and she wasn't nice about it at all, not even a little bit. She threw her voice back and forth, acting like two different people who were asking and then answering questions about Christianity.

"Why did Jesus have to die?" Captain TTL asked.

"Because of our sinfulness," Captain TTL answered.

On and on Captain TTL went like this, busting out questions and answers until finally the Christians really had nothing to say. (To their credit, the Christians did try to throw out a few answers different from the ones Captain TTL was giving. But in the end, none of the answers proved that any of the Christians had the ability to interpret and explain the how-it-all-works theology behind the questions Captain TTL was debating.)

So slowly the Christians retreated, determined to regroup for round two. Cam didn't know it, but the Christians apparently retreated straight to their on-campus ministry leader, Paul. They told him all about Captain TTL and what went down in class. They explained all the beliefs they had unsuccessfully tried to defend and how they wanted to get back in there to prove what they knew was true about their faith. So Paul laid out new arguments about the questions

Captain TTL had brought up since he was always able to work up newer, better, fresher answers the Christians could borrow.

And so back the Christians went for round two, unloading Paul's answers on Captain TTL and her boat of philosophizers. Paul's new arguments were huge. They sank the doubters' boat in no time flat, totally ruffled feathers, and caused a bunch of static that left Captain TTL silent. After all, the stuff the Christians unleashed on Captain TTL was new to her. It was full of interpretations and explanations she'd never heard before (or maybe missed since having ditched Christianity a while back).

Not knowing what to do with the info the Christians dished out—and not wanting to look anything less than totally right and totally in control no matter what was actually going on—Captain TTL decided it was time to retreat. But instead of admitting she'd been whipped, she just pretended the debate was so incredibly lame in the first place that it wasn't even worth talking about anymore. And with that, Captain TTL muttered something like, "As if anyone is still debating this anyway," and commanded her boat to sail away into the semester, done with that particular argument.

The Christians celebrated their victory, which led to a huge campuswide push for Christians of all kinds to speak up for their beliefs. But the Christians hadn't really come as far as they thought. Well, at least not in Cam's opinion. They were still in their boat, paddling forward with the help of beliefs that were borrowed from someone else.

So as much as it was tight to see Captain TTL row away into the sunset and see Christians all over campus psyched to make a big statement about their faith, Cam wanted something more. Faith might begin with an older Christian passing along beliefs, but at some point Cam realized all Christians needed to become the official owners of their faith. That was the only way Cam's faith could become personal and something solid enough to last a lifetime.

That's where the hard work began for Cam. Through mentorship and study, about a zillion hours spent asking questions, and almost the same amount of time spent in prayer, the how-it-all-works level of Cam's faith began to take shape. Best of all, Cam now felt confident saying, "I don't know," instead of struggling to defend the Christian faith with a set of borrowed beliefs. Cam had learned that owning one's faith isn't about knowing all the answers. It is about spending the energy and time it takes to understand the truths behind the answers and therefore the beliefs. It is about dedicating one's life to those truths.

BELIEFS GOOD ENOUGH TO OWN

This quiz will help you own your core Christian beliefs.

Cam was stuck in a hard place, forced to realize how Christian belief has to be owned by each individual Christian in order for a lifetime of faith to make sense, feel personal, and promote spiritual growth. The whole situation was a wake-up call, and so is this quiz.

This quiz pairs beliefs with different passages from Scripture. Before you choose an answer, own it. Read all the Scripture references, and don't choose an answer until you can explain to yourself how the answer you've picked fits with the Scripture references. When you're done, check out what your answers mean at the end of the quiz.

1. The Bible . . .
2 Timothy 3:14—17 | Psalm 119:89—93
2 Samuel 22:31—37

A Contains all the truth God wants us to know and can be read literally.

B Is directly inspired by the Holy Spirit and is the basis of Christian belief, but is more sacred than it is literal.

C Is infallible and read literally because it's the final authority.

D Needs to be interpreted by Christians using God's gift of reason since it's full of truth but written for a different culture, time, and place.

2. What's your opinion: Can women lead churches?

Judges 4:1—9 | 1 Timothy 2:11—12
Galatians 3:28 | 1 Corinthians 11:1—10

A Men are the traditional leaders of the church, but it's clear women should play a central role too.

B Men should carry on the traditions of the priesthood, just as Christ fulfilled that role in His time.

C Women are amazing speakers and inspirational leaders who can channel God's message and reveal His will, but men should run the church.

D Leadership isn't as important as fellowship, so anyone can lead others to get in touch with Christ through their faith, life, and attitude.

3. Salvation and the ability to overcome all things in Christ come from . . .

Ephesians 2:8—9 | Revelation 3:20
Acts 2:38—43 | John 3:5—6

A Accepting Jesus into your heart and being baptized if your church is into that.

B A personal relationship with Christ and being baptized according to the requirements of the church.

C Accepting Jesus into your heart and receiving the baptism of the Holy Spirit.

D A personal relationship with Christ, centered on spiritual growth.

28

4. Agree or disagree: Satan is a literal being that interferes with our Christian walk.

Luke 4:1—13 | Acts 5:1—5 | Luke 13:11—16
Revelation 12:7—17

A Satan is real. His actions affect our lives, but he doesn't directly possess or corrupt us very often.

B Satan is more an evil force or influence in the world—tempting and leading us astray—than he is a literal being.

C Satan is a literal being. He and other demons are always trying to corrupt or possess us.

D Satan's image is powerful—so whether he's real or not, evil in the world comes as a result of the negativity and corruption associated with Satan.

5. The Holy Spirit . . .

Acts 2:1—21 | 1 Corinthians 6:1—11
Joel 2:28—29 | 1 John 5:6—9

A Convicts us, fills us, and leads us.

B Is a mystery we can't really explain, but works to guide us.

C Lives in us and is seen through miraculous gifts when people become spiritually mature.

D Is a presence of God individual believers can feel, be led by, and be filled with.

ANSWERS

If you picked mostly **A** answers, your best route to owning your faith is to go at Christianity through conservative yet varied views about the Bible. Focus on Scripture and on the Jesus who speaks to you from the pages of the Gospels.

If you picked mostly **B** answers, your best route to owning your faith is to go at Christianity through the essence of Scripture. Quiet yourself so you can tap into sacred themes of the Bible, as they've inspired spiritual growth in Christians for centuries, rather than use the Bible as a literal answer book.

If you picked mostly **C** answers, your best route to owning your faith is to go at Christianity through outward expression and inward spiritual growth. Stick with your conservative views about faith and the Bible, but get active with your expression of these beliefs, letting yourself be open to healing and other spiritual gifts as you mature in Christ.

If you picked mostly **D** answers, your best route to owning your faith is to go at Christianity through moderation. Combine a bit of faith's mystery with a bit of logic and reason to come up with a confident set of beliefs that are true to Christianity's core but modern enough for your life in the current era.

3

The Flip Side

Getting into Your Faith by Learning about Others

Maybe you've never thought much about it, but understanding other kinds of Christians can help you firm up your own beliefs. How? By finding an answer to the question: What are other Christians doing out there on God's bigger scene?

One way to do this is to visit different churches, which, let's say, you and a friend decide to do. The first one you decide to check out is the megachurch—since you've heard good things about all the small groups, classes, and events that go on at big churches.

THE MEGACHURCH

Parking is maybe not the easiest thing when you and your friend roll up, but you eventually spot someone pulling out and you pull in to take their spot. A quick 360: Church building . . . BIG. Parking lot . . . BIG. Crowd . . . BIG. And just as you swing around, giving the car door a good slam shut, you notice a BIG group of people walking by giving you and your friend the "What's up?" head nod. So you guys "Hey!" the people back with a head nod of your own, grab your Bibles off the top of the car, and start toward the main sanctuary.

Inside, you wander around for a long time. Mostly the two of you want to lay low and away from places where you might stick out as obvious newbies. You decide that a pair of seats about halfway to the left are just about right. You can see the overhead great. And though the stage is a bit off-center from where you're sitting, you've heard it'll be no big deal since the pastor is going to walk around rather than just stand in one place.

After the worship band covers everything from regular stuff like "Our God Is an Awesome God" to newer stuff like the latest Jeremy Camp song, the pastor makes his way up to the stage. The guy is sort of dad-aged and wears casual stuff you'd see any guy wearing any day of the week. He gets through the announcements in the bulletin, asks people to give a quick hug and hello to the person sitting next to them, and then goes right into the sermon.

The sermon is really organized. Just a few Gospel verses are the focus, but most every reference outside those Scriptures is to New Testament stories and ideas you find easy to understand. The sermon comes to a close as you and your friend get to the last fill-in-the-blank lines of your sermon outlines. Then there's a quick prayer and a shout-out to first-time visitors like yourselves to fill out a card so the church can get someone in touch with you later. It's a we'll-call-you kind of deal.

All in all, the megachurch vibe was comfortable; the atmosphere was positive and

Tons of groups, classes, and events

friendly, the sermon was easy to follow, and everything was relaxed and social instead of being stuffy, traditional, or really serious. There were so many people there, you and your friend didn't stick out at all, and there weren't any awkward conversations with strangers that left you guys wondering what to say next. When it all wrapped up, there wasn't any pressure to join up with the church right then and there. Plus, the church had tons of groups, classes, and events to get involved with, including a smaller home-church movement in case you were the kind of person who preferred that to doing the big-sanctuary thing.

THE SMALL CHURCH

The next church you and your friend visit is much smaller. It's a neighborhood church, so the parking lot isn't quite the shopping-mall type scene you found at the megachurch. But you do happen to pull in alongside people who say hello. A family hops out of their car and the mom and dad strike up a conversation with you immediately, since it's pretty obvious you're not regular church members. The family is cool for the most part, chatting it up just enough to make you both feel welcome but not weirded-out.

The sanctuary is a lot smaller than you thought it would be, causing you and your friend to give each other a nervous glance. It's gonna be hard to hide from the new visitor stand-up-and-wave routine (if the church is into that kind of thing). So after some quick mental calculating about which seats will most definitely be outside the pastor's line of sight, the two of you find yourselves plopping down somewhere toward the middle in a couple of seats just at the edge of the aisle. An usher who's passing out bulletins says "Hi!"—but it's nothing pushy. He just asks a couple of polite questions about why you came today and then wishes you a nice visit. As he walks away, you and your friend wait for the service to start, feeling good about what's gone on so far.

Things get rolling with singing. Then you listen to a few announcements, take a minute to pray, and everything is brought down to a level that's a bit more hushed—a sure sign it's sermon time. It turns out there's no step-by-step follow along, though. It's all about flipping from Old to New Testament passages to keep up with the pastor's overall message. So you both get with the flipping and wield blazing pens in order to scribble as many notes as you can before it's off to a new part of Scripture and more info about the day's overall message. You both get that all the verses seem to back one another up as a way to prove the truth of the pastor's bigger message, but the whole thing ends up taking longer than what you're used to. It's nothing you and your friend can't handle, but not what goes down where you two go to church. Your services are based more on biblical themes than on specific Scripture references, meaning you can tell one of the main goals at the small church is solid, in-depth biblical study. Nothing is watered down or made easy for the sake of convenience.

After the sermon wraps up, the trip back to the car is full of lots of "Hi's," "Hello's," and "Nice to meet you's." Seems like almost everyone wants to shake your hand, ask how you found the service today, or invite you to the all-church potluck that starts in an hour or so. So the vibe is definitely more intimate than the megachurch. It's more community-based and feels comfy, with just enough people to make things feel social but just few enough people to give it a family-kind of vibe.

THE TRADITIONAL CHURCH

The third church you visit—the traditional one—has a lot of the same qualities as the other two churches. It's got a positive vibe and straightforward preaching like the megachurch, but the vibe comes from different stuff. It comes from all the visuals that surround you, from stained-glass windows to cool architecture to altar paintings. Things feel more like the kind of church you see in beautiful pictures of a friend's "amazing" trip to Europe or in art books about the history of the church. As for similarities with the neighborhood church, the traditional one is

Community-based with a family kind of vibe

kind of the same size in terms of the number of people there, but what people are doing makes the traditional church a bit different—they're doing nothing. Just sitting, and it's really, really quiet—which sort of weirds you and your friend out at first.

After you stop worrying about making too much noise, the weirded-out feeling passes. The two of you start to notice how refreshing it is to be someplace without all the chitchat and background noise that always turn up in regular life. It makes the traditional church feel like something special or sacred. Some people say "Hi!" to one another as they pass, but most just walk to a pew and sit down, sitting in silence for a while to center themselves before the service begins. It's a kind of pre-service routine here to just finally chill out, let things go, and try to prepare yourself to be open to God. The body is calmed, the mind is quieted, and it's a time when a kind of peace sweeps over you in the stillness.

The service starts with music booming through the church in a big way. Apparently the place has an organ in the back, and when the pipes start blowing, people begin to crack open their hymnals and sing old-school lyrics with a lot of "ye," "thou," and "art" type words. As you guys join in with the singing you notice the church leaders enter and begin to prepare things, so you guys open your Bibles and wait, thinking it's sermon time. People all around you are opening a book too, but it's not the Bible. Your friend pulls one of the books from the back of the pew in front of you and opens it, trying to figure out what's going on. Turns out, the books are full of prayer-type stuff. The church leader says one part, and the people read their part back by using what's written in the book. The two of you fidget and flounder over the prayer book enough that the guy next to you notices. He reaches to help by thumbing over to the right page so you can say the prayer too. He also nods in the direction of today's bulletin, which apparently has the prayer book page numbers listed. Since you guys are new to the whole prayer book thing in general, the numbers didn't really have a connection until he pointed this out.

Next everyone listens to a speaker read two passages from the Bible—one from the Old Testament and one from the New. The priest's sermon uses the main points of these readings but also goes into a discussion about some church father who wrote a lot about Christianity way back when, and how we can impact society by following his example. You and your friend jot down the church father's name with a little note to look him up and keep following along with the priest's train of thought. But for the most part, you just listen to what he's got to say about ways faith and life can intersect. And when it's all said and done, the service wraps up with a blessing over the crowd and that's that.

Quiet, sacred atmosphere

The more "churchy" feel of the place, combined with the quiet, was way different from the other two churches you visited, but the traditional church didn't disappoint. The sermon was clear, the people seemed cool, and there was the same kind of good, positive vibe as in the other two churches. Things weren't quite as social, but the environment was unique and really refreshing.

THE CONCLUSION

Looking back at the megachurch, the small church, and the traditional church, each is set up to offer Christians a different kind of experience, but connecting with God is always the goal. No matter which experience provides the best connection for you, knowing what works will help firm up your beliefs. To summarize:

- At the megachurch, BIG described everything, including the vibe. Big choices in terms of stuff to do. Big social scene in terms of people to hang with. But it was so big that it would be difficult to know everyone on a personal level.
- At the small church, there was more of a family kind of vibe. Everyone tended to know one another on a more personal level. The social scene was more limited than the megachurch's scene, but was friendly and comfy.

- At the traditional church, there was a community kind of vibe. Like the small church, it had a small membership compared to a megachurch. The traditional wasn't as social as the megachurch or small church. Members focused more on their quiet, individual connections with God.

WHAT'S A STATEMENT OF FAITH (SOF)?

The vibe each church gives off is directly related to how the Christians who worship there read the Bible and what's summed up in the church's statement of faith (SOF). The SOF is the set of beliefs a church is built upon. So if you look at the SOF, it'll help make sense of the vibe you're getting because the SOF lists the priorities of the church right up front. For example, you visit a church and read this:

> Our theology is not innovative—anyone familiar with historic Christian doctrine will find that these statements fall in the center of evangelical theology (evangelical means theology derived from the evangel, or the Gospel; in other words, it's biblical theology rather than speculative theology or theology rooted in tradition). We try not to be dogmatic about matters on which Bible-based believers have held divergent views. We want our core beliefs to be centered in Christ and His message as found in and supported by the clearest passages of Scripture.

"Okay," you say, "that's great. But what does it mean?" If you take it line-by-line, you'll know. The first thing we get is info about the kind of theology going on at this church. Nothing at the church is gonna be based on complicated discussions, debates, or church traditions. It'll be straightforward Matthew, Mark, Luke, and John info. The church doesn't want to preach about stuff that divides Christians, so it's safe to say you're not going to get a sermon that debates this or that verse or insists on what a passage of Scripture really, *really* means. It won't be a confrontational, stuffy, or traditional vibe at all.

Reading a church's SOF is a totally doable thing. Once you know what to look for, you can get the hang of it pretty quick. Just keep these points in mind:

- Whether a church is mega, small, or traditional doesn't matter. SOFs are individual to each church, no matter how similar (or different) two churches seem.
- If you haven't read through your church's SOF, it's like being in a long-term relationship just based on somebody's looks. You've got to know what's below the surface too.
- Reading the SOF will tell you if the vibe you're feeling is founded on beliefs you agree with.

Do you know what statements of faith your church stands for?

The only other thing to know about a church's SOF is where to find it.

First, you can check the Sunday bulletin or sermon outline. Sometimes the SOF is printed on the back. If you see a quick little list of beliefs, you've got it. Most times the SOF will just be a list of sentences all starting with phrases like, "We believe . . ." or "We trust that . . ."

Second, you might find the SOF wound into a ministory. So it'd be like you start with something like "Jesus proclaimed the reign of God and then . . . ," and the story would go on to state all the things Jesus did. Each of those things is one belief the church is founded on. It's a statement of what the church believes about Jesus, or about anything else in Christianity, like salvation, the end times, Creation, the Holy Spirit, or whatever.

Third, the SOF may be its own deal, tucked inside a welcome packet or available as a single piece of paper you can pick up from the main church office. Ask an usher or zip by the main church office to get one.

Fourth, you can do the online thing. Most churches that have websites include a space for their SOF. All you have to do is find the "what we believe" link and give it a click.

TUNING IN TO CHURCH VIBES

This quiz will help you see what's behind the Christian vibes you're most comfortable around.

Churches all give off a different vibe because each has a different idea of the kind of worship that'll highlight the beliefs of that particular group and make worshipers feel comfortable they're connecting with God in a way that relates to their beliefs. The foundation of each church is wrapped up in its statement of faith, which lays out what's key to that community of believers.

How well do you understand your own beliefs? Answer the questions below. Check out your answers at the end of the quiz.

1. Which Bible translation do you prefer to use?

A New International Version (NIV), Holman Christian Standard (HCSB), or New American Standard (NASB).

B New American (NAB) or the New/Revised Standard (RSV, NRSV).

C King James (KJV).

D The one that makes the most sense to you.

2. How would you describe God?

A A personal Being who is all-knowing, all-loving, and all-wise. He sent His Son to die for our sins.

B Our divine Parent, who created us, loves us, provides for us, and guides us.

C The one true and living God who is worthy of all obedience, honor, and love, and is perfect in every way.

D A friend, father, and leader for our lives.

3. What does salvation do to a person's heart and mind?

A Salvation means you're born again. Jesus forgives you for your sin, and you're able to focus on Him as a way to follow God in all things.

B Salvation means you've died to sin. This lets your charity become more genuine and your love become more unconditional.

C Salvation means you're separated from the evil in your life. You can mature spiritually to become as holy as God expects Christians to be.

D Salvation means you've understood Jesus in your life and are no longer separated from the spiritual growth He has planned for you.

4. What's the clearest way to show people the reality of God's love?

A Evangelism and missions trips.

B Charity and service work.

C Healing and miracles.

D The way we live our lives.

5. Which description of Christian fellowship is the most meaningful to you?

A A gathering of believers who want to serve, praise, and worship our Lord.

B A gathering of believers and people who desire God's sacred guidance.

C A gathering of believers freed from sin and restored by the Holy Spirit.

D A gathering of believers who don't fight over differences but instead choose to work together.

ANSWERS

If you picked mostly **A** answers, the statements of faith (SOF) you'll be interested in will emphasize the role of Jesus and the gospel message. Read through the profiles in the **ROSE**-colored section in Part Two to see all the different kinds of Christian groups that give off this vibe.

If you picked mostly **B** answers, the SOFs you'll be interested in will emphasize the role of charity, unity, and other Christian virtues. Read through the profiles in the **TEAL**-colored section in Part Two to see all the different kinds of Christian groups that give off this vibe.

If you picked mostly **C** answers, the SOFs you'll be interested in will emphasize the role of the Holy Spirit. Read through the profiles in the **BLUE**-colored section in Part Two to see all the different kinds of Christian groups that give off this vibe.

If you picked mostly **D** answers, the SOFs you'll be interested in will emphasize the responsibility of the individual in society. Read through the profiles in the **PURPLE**-colored section in Part Two to see all the different kinds of Christian groups that give off this vibe.

Huge, Hushed, or What?!

Different Kinds of Churches

Each kind of Christianity is distinct. So it's only natural that the worship experience you'd have at each church would be distinct too. Pastors and priests know there's a people pattern when it comes to Christians. Each Christian has a set of things he or she is looking for in order to be comfortable with a church. And most often, Christians are looking for a church that looks a lot like they do. They're looking for a people pattern they recognize and that matches up to the way they see themselves—like an outgoing person being into a church that's really social, while an introverted person might be more into a church that's low-key. Comfort level is important, so when you spot your people pattern at a church, it'll make things a hundred times easier to get involved and grow spiritually.

So let's run through some of the things that create a people pattern at any given church. We'll do music, size, age, race, and ethnicity.

MUSIC

Music is one of the most powerful tools Christians can use to connect with God, and the kind of music you like says something about the kind of Christian experience you crave. Some Christians like music to be the same no matter where they're at. This would be those who are into alternative music and don't really like that much else, so they intentionally stick with a church where alternative music is played at least part of the time. That way things are always comfortable since the music is familiar, easy to learn, and stuff the person likes singing along to. Other Christians are the total opposite. They don't want to hear the same thing at church that they listen to in other places. They want church music to be set apart so worship ends up being something different, special, or a kind of break from the ordinary grind. This kind of Christian might be the guy or girl who does country music during the week but likes hymns or choir music or organs or chanting or maybe even no music at all when it comes to getting serious with God.

Church music isn't made to order, though. It usually just comes down to the money a church can spend on music and the number of people willing to volunteer. So that means you might have to compromise on music to get other things you're looking for in a church. For example, I used to switch off between two churches. One had way better music, but most of the people I knew there were just casual friends. The other church had all my long-term friends, but some seriously not-my-style music. I didn't see my people pattern in it at all. Not much could be done, though, since

Ever tried letting music guide your prayers?

the guy in charge of music didn't get all that much help. The only other person who made the scene to help him out was this girl, who was there every week without fail, so the two of them could only do so much. Without more volunteers or a bigger music budget, the church played the kind of music it *could* play, not the kind it might have *liked* to play.

You might also want to keep two other points about music in mind:

First, people who run churches try to please the majority. So even if your church can only come up with one music volunteer, and he's some guy who loves to play the bagpipes, the guy is going to at least try to play songs the majority of people like instead of experimenting with new stuff. After all, worship is about being able to connect to God, and church music is supposed to enhance this connection for the most people possible.

Second, lots of churches follow tradition when it comes to music. The deal at churches like this is still about connecting with God, but a lot of the connection is done through words, prayer, or silence instead of catchy tunes. So you might hear hymns, spirituals, or songs that go back into Christianity's past and are sung as a kind of prayer rather than a bunch of music played just to get people up and into a catchy beat or hook.

SIZE

We can skip right past clichés here since we know good things don't always come in small packages and that bigger isn't always better. To be real about it, church size is a practical matter between you and God; that's it. You'll find your people pattern pretty easily when you ask yourself these basic questions:

- How many people do I like to have around when I want to worship?
- Can I connect with God if church is a quiet place with only a few people at the service each week?
- Do I feel embarrassed to praise God in front of a bunch of others?

Probably the most important thing about church size is whether or not you're getting into the kinds of relationships you want. Relationships you have with people at church are tied to the community's size. To understand more about the two sides of the coin at different-size churches, check out the charts on the next three pages.

CHURCH SIZES

CHURCH SIZE	COOL	NOT COOL
SMALLER CHURCH Less than or in the 100s of people every week.	1. People know people.	1. People are up in other people's business.
	2. The dependability factor: You won't be surprised by curve balls about where the church is going—since it's small enough to know what's up.	2. The boredom factor. For real . . . there's only so many times you'll want to sing that same song.
	3. Mentorship doubles as friendship, which might make spiritual growth easier or more rewarding.	3. Mentors are people you know, meaning there's some chance your secrets might leak out.
	4. More control over what's going on in your church community.	4. Opportunity for bossy or controlling people to take hold of everything.
	5. Worship environment that's more like a living room with friends than a stuffy or formal church.	5. Nowhere to disappear when you're not in the mood to socialize.
	6. Usually at least one Bible study or small-group class to get involved with.	6. Get tired of the same Bible study teachers.

CHURCH SIZES

CHURCH SIZE	COOL	NOT COOL
MEDIUM CHURCH In the 200–500 people range every week.	1. Enough people that you don't have to limit your circle of friends.	1. Just enough new people to keep you meeting but not really getting to know people down deep.
	2. Different Christian perspectives because you've got more than one pastor.	2. Getting hooked on one pastor and starting to play favorites.
	3. Big churchwide efforts that aren't just about religion, like garage sales or picnics.	3. Only one big trip, event, or thing going on at any one time.
	4. More places to volunteer or get involved in the church directly.	4. More church management, committees, and less individual control over what's going on.
	5. Large enough sanctuary to keep to yourself if you want to during the service.	5. Sanctuary still small enough that people will notice you're off on your own.
	6. Enough church leaders to have a few regular groups.	6. Classes are well run, but the same things are taught over and over again by different volunteers.

CHURCH SIZES

CHURCH SIZE	COOL	NOT COOL
BIG CHURCH More than 500 and into the 1,000s of people every week	1. Tons of people and lots of clubs, groups, trips, classes, or ways to meet others.	1. So many choices it becomes overwhelming and seems like a lot of work to get involved in anything or meet anyone.
	2. More types of missions, outreach, ministry, and evangelism opportunities to be involved with.	2. Not putting that much importance on getting into outreach because it seems like you can always do it later.
	3. Big pastoral staff for support, teaching, guidance, etc.	3. So many people to minister to, nobody has time to mentor for a long period of time.
	4. Sanctuary so big you can sit with whole groups of friends.	4. Sanctuary so crowded or loud you miss important info or get distracted.
	5. Events and classes run by church volunteers who come up with new topics all the time.	5. Unorganized events or classes because volunteer leaders aren't prepped or trained well enough.

AGE

Whom do you want to worship with most: people your age, your parents' age, your grandparents' age, or some kind of mix? The average age of people at any given church is actually pretty tightly connected to where a church is located. For example:

- A church near a bunch of elementary or junior high schools will probably have a good number of mom- and dad-aged people who've got young kids.
- A church located near a college campus will probably have a good number of twenty-somethings.
- A church near a big retirement community will probably have lots of senior citizens.

The real surprise when it comes to age is actually how irrelevant it can be. It might seem like you've found your people pattern at a church full of people close to your age, but a lot of us are young in terms of age but a lot older in our approach to spirituality, general outlook on life, or vice versa. Age also ends up being less important if we like the security or support we get from a church we've been at for years, even if most of the people aren't our age. And age could be no big deal if the most important thing to our spiritual growth is mentorship and teaming up with older Christians in order to learn life lessons and grow.

So the age factor is more a comfort-level thing than any kind of magic number that translates into an exact fit. Church will be most comfortable if you find a balance between people you can kick it with and people you can learn from. Some church communities have both kinds of people, all within a few years of your own age. Others have both kinds of people, and you'll end up with friends from your generation, but from many other generations too. Finding the right balance is a lot like finding the right kind of music. All churches will have barriers or limits they can't do anything about. So if you live in a town that's only got about one thousand people in it, it's not really the church's fault if there's not a good mix of ages going on in the congregation. There are only so many people in the area, right? Who shows up is who shows up. So a church has to set up the worship experience for that particular crowd of people, no matter what age they might be.

RACE AND ETHNICITY

It's always hard to talk about race or ethnicity because nobody wants to hurt anyone's feelings or say something stupid or insensitive. Depending on the kind of church you and your family attend, what part of the country you live in, or what your parents have taught you about people from other cultures, you've probably already got some views about race and about the cultural stuff that makes up ethnicity.

You may even hold stereotypes about these things. Stereotypes are incomplete judgments based on random bits and pieces of a bigger picture. They're when we think of everyone in a certain group as the same, based on some oversimplified, general characteristics, because we don't know the real info or haven't tried to figure it out.

Things like stereotypes make our race-and-ethnicity people pattern a hard thing to get beyond. That said, the point here isn't to get anyone to adopt a new ethnicity or tap into a new culture just for the sake of having done it. Rather it's to ask ourselves this question: Have I ever considered race, ethnicity, or culture as a factor that might have something to do with learning more about Christianity in general?

The answer to this question will impact your faith. Different cultures grow up with different tastes and traditions, and those are incorporated into the church. So it's no surprise that a lot of things that separate one kind of Christianity from another are based on these preferences. Everything—from the colors a church uses to decorate, the kind of food served after service, the way people are baptized, or even the kind of missions

Why is it easier to stereotype people we don't know?

work a church does—can have some link to the race, ethnicity, or cultural background of a church. For example:

- Music that ties people back to their history or roots emphasizes pride in a person's heritage. For example, the gospel music or spirituals used in many African-American churches celebrate forms of music that began within the African-American community.

- Social-outreach programs that cater to a specific ethnic community help establish stability. For example, a Christian church with a lot of Hispanic members may gear their outreach toward Spanish-speaking countries or toward helping new Hispanic immigrants settle in America.

- Evangelism that centers on certain parts of the globe seeks to bring Christ to new places. For example, a Disciples of Christ church with lots of Asian-American members might concentrate donations and missions resources toward ministry work in places like China or Japan.

A church's connection between Christianity and race or ethnicity can be strong or weak, depending on its membership. If it's strong, you'll see a clear line of influence.

Race and ethnicity also will factor into your faith on a personal comfort level. On this level, the truth is that each of us knows we feel more comfortable around certain kinds of people than we do around others. It's just an internal feeling you get that makes you feel like "Yeah, this is where I fit." It's like a best-friend kind of thing—you feel comfortable and know you can be yourself around a best friend. You know what to expect from the kind of beliefs they've got, the foods they like, and the stuff they do for fun. Race and ethnicity are the same deal. You'll know where you click—where you see your people pattern.

YOUR PEOPLE PATTERN

The quiz below will help you figure out your people pattern.

We each see ourselves in the kind of Christianity we practice, so keep the picture clear by being aware of your people patterns—in music, size, age, race, and ethnicity.

Read the questions below, then check out what your answers mean at the end of the quiz.

1. **I like being in a social group that's full of people who . . .**

   A At least ask what's been up if they haven't seen me all week.

   B Say regular hellos, but let me keep to myself if I choose.

   C Want to hang, swap stories, or stay after to chat it up.

   D Like to mix up our social group by hanging with other kinds of believers.

2. I'd like to go to a church where most people dress . . .

A In what they'd wear every day.

B In something a little nicer than normal.

C In church clothes.

D In things that are comfy, but nice.

3. Little kids hanging around in the service. What's your take?

A Little kids aren't really going to get what's going on and can be distracting. It's better if they have a separate service that's more on their level.

B Little kids learn stuff when they stay in church with you. Staying lets them see more of what's going on, and it's more of a family vibe that way.

C Little kids aren't that big a deal. People are going to be making noise praising and worshiping anyway. Kids could go, but no one would really be bothered if they stayed.

D Little kids can be included in worship if people are willing to get creative and break out of the norm when it comes to the church service.

4. Is it cool to mix up musical styles at church, doing some new stuff and some old stuff?

A Sure, why not? I have favorites, but it's okay if we don't always get to them.

B It's not a big deal, but certain songs really make it seem like church, so it's good if those songs can stay constant.

C Music is so powerful, but it's about the lyrics mostly—so I wouldn't want to mess with those.

D It's great when Christians can switch from traditional to something that puts a twist into worship.

5. I relate to people who want their church to . . .

A Be independent, with no bigger organization running each church.

B Preserve Christianity's history.

C Be a community center for inspiration.

D Be a source of social change.

ANSWERS

If you picked mostly **A** answers, you're looking for social, independent people patterns at a church. Understanding more about your faith comes easiest for you when you're at a church where people help one another adapt, change, and grow as a group.

If you picked mostly **B** answers, you're looking for a people pattern different from the other things you do all week. It's important to you that your faith stand out and be set apart from what's ordinary in your life as a way to create a space for your spirituality.

If you picked mostly **C** answers, you're looking for a comfortable people pattern you can participate in—one that you can feel. Expressions of faith help you discover the potential lying within each person and promote spiritual growth.

If you picked mostly **D** answers, you're looking for a people pattern that's flexible enough to change, but keeps its focus on uniting Christians across age, race, or other factors.

5

Divine Connections

Let's say you've gone to a church with a friend or relative, and it's different from what you're used to. Or perhaps you don't have a church home and you're looking for one. One of the worst things about going to a new church is the anticipation. Everybody is standing there all confident in what they're doing, and you don't know what comes next. So it'll be like you're standing there alongside everybody trying to figure it out. Then suddenly you're the only one standing because everyone else has knelt down and you missed the tip-off clue to kneel.

These situations are inevitable because church services are all a little bit different. The things that are used or done at a service won't be the same from place to place. It's personalized for each kind of Christianity or each local church. Although these situations might be awkward, sometimes they can lead you to experiences that deepen your connection to God. This happened to me at a friend's wedding one time. I left the wedding exposed to things I'd never thought about in terms of connecting with God, but I was so out of place that at first it was classic "Hi! . . . Can you say, dork?!" I wasn't even out of the car more than five minutes before I felt like the word *newbie* was flashing across my forehead.

It was a traditional Greek Orthodox wedding. It

wasn't as traditional as an Orthodox wedding can be, but let's just put it this way . . . my outfit wasn't even close to traditional. I can only thank God's fashion savvy in my life that morning that I didn't feel led by the Spirit to reach for a pair of slacks (a serious no-no for girls in many Orthodox communities). But alas, God still thought He'd have some fun with me, I guess, and didn't send fire from the sky to stop me from showing up at the wedding wearing a dress that was so horribly wrong it was hilarious.

So, after some disapproving stares and a lot of giggles by little six-year-old girls who were smart enough to have worn the "right" kind of dresses, I made my way into the church. The place was tight! I just couldn't help staring in awe since my own church wasn't really an official church kind of building, but more like, um . . . a high-school gym. Our sanctuary was the basketball court, and our youth group met in the school's band room. I mean, the band room had some pretty sweet new carpet and whatnot, but needless to say, we didn't really have the sweeping ceilings that the Orthodox church had. We didn't have the tiled artwork, or the painted altar screens, or the . . . well, I could go on and on. Our preacher delivered his sermons with a plug-in mic and a carry-around amp. Not that that's shabby or whatever, but can you blame me for staring at the other church?

How often do you get outside your comfort zone?

All my staring got me a bit off track. I wasn't paying attention to what people were doing and took a seat toward the back. So you know how the back of a big church is usually the empty place to sit? Well, it was the same deal here. It was empty, but so was most of the rest of the church. You'd think the ghost-town vibe would have given me a clue about what was going on, but it didn't. I just kept sitting there, figuring people would come inside after they'd chatted a bit out front. Turns out there was some kind of prewedding blessing of the marriage rings going on outside the church doors. Whether traditional or not, all the wedding guests (minus one) were outside to watch this ring blessing before the priest led the bride and groom inside. I saw people hanging out by the doors when I came in, but I thought that's all they were doing—hanging out.

Anyway, it all got sorted out and everybody ended up back inside the church, but I still had a lot to learn about the style of an Orthodox service. Within minutes the whole place was full of smoke. I did my best to look like it was all good and that I wasn't about to totally pass out from the smell. A guy kept wandering around the church swinging a ball of incense back and forth, and I'm not kidding you, I could barely see the row ahead of me when the incense guy was all done. Eventually the incense did clear, but then I had no idea what I was looking at. There was a crowning of the bride and groom and some circling around an altar, but I couldn't figure out where we were in the ceremony because there were no "I do's." Nobody was promising to love, honor, or cherish, or anything like that. Turns out there was never going to be any loving, honoring, or cherishing either. The wedding services for most Orthodox Christians don't include it. So I was sitting there getting all fidgety and thinking, *How much longer until they get to the "I do"*?! I didn't realize it, but the service was almost over.

In the end, I not only made it through the entire wedding without totally ruining anything for the bride and groom, but I also took a lot of what I experienced away with me. The dark interior of the church made me feel small and more able to appreciate how big God is. The art was beautiful. And even though I almost choked on the incense at first, I found that I really like services to have something distinct about them, like the smell of the incense. It creates a kind of memory between the service and how I felt being there. I found new things a Christian like me can use to connect with God.

So the things done or used in a church service matter. And though we might not be a part of a particular kind of Christianity, new things we experience on a visit can enhance our connection to God.

In the following four sections are some of the things you might see used or done in different church services.

1. TRADITION

If a church uses or does things in a traditional way, you'll know right from the start. Tall hats. People in flowing robes. Colored or embroidered sashes. Altars and screens and a lot going on up front. Slow and careful movement. And of course . . . white collars. Any of these things are a tip-off about what you're in for, meaning that whatever you're about to experience is gonna be formal and done just like it's been done for ages. Things will be organized, consistent, and, most of all, historical. When tradition is used at a church service, it connects believers with God by reminding them of the bigger Christian picture with all its history, people, and rituals.

Church leaders take care of most everything when traditional things are done or used at a church service, so you won't be handling or touching a lot of stuff. That part is tradition too: Some people are leaders trained to perform and preserve the rituals of Christianity; other people are worshipers. But the church can educate people to become leaders on some level so nobody is locked into any one role.

Doing the tradition thing also means using art. Things like stained glass, icons, or paintings surround worshipers and are used for two reasons:

First, art is a way to remind people where to keep their focus. For example, a stained-glass window featuring a Bible story connects believers back to God's Word. Icons that can be held lead a worshiper into thoughts of respect for God or for Christians who've come before. People don't pray to the icon. They use the icon to focus the mind in prayer, like a kind of entry into a spiritual place in the soul.

Second, art sets a kind of mood. The way a church is decorated makes you feel a certain way inside. And services that use tradition like to put art right up front to give an overall mood even before anything is said or done.

Doing or using traditional things in services is almost like giving Christians a way to travel through time. Huge sweeping cathedrals, art, formal rituals, or being able to hear the Bible read in an ancient language makes the past seem really fresh, like it's right there for you to grab.

2. VOLUNTEERISM

If a church uses or does things by making use of volunteers, it creates a service that's really accessible. You don't have to know or do anything special to participate. You just have to want to worship. That's it.

Doing a service that includes volunteers leads to lots of creative input from church

Is art something you consider spiritually uplifting?

members. Services end up being a reflection of the kinds of people in the church membership, because the membership is heavily involved in all parts of any service. It's the volunteers who help to fill established roles in the service, like leading a prayer or reading a passage of Scripture, or who help in other ways, like playing music, taking collections, offering small groups or classes for growth, running missions trips, and even doing things you probably never think about—such as buying paper towels for the bathrooms or deciding if it's bagels or donuts on the tables after church. Pastors still present the sermon and are in charge of leading everyone on a spiritual level, but for other stuff it's welcomed and/or necessary that people from the congregation get involved.

This leads to really flexible services. Things can be changed around, made longer or shorter, or updated to include new stuff. Even big rituals, like a wedding, for example, are flexible and creative at a church that does the volunteer thing. So it'd be like a couple saying they wanted to get married and then their pastor telling them, "Cool. Why don't you create your own ceremony, tell me what parts of the Bible really inspire you, and then I'll put it all together. Okay?" The whole thing becomes a kind of creative project for everybody involved.

When churches use or do things based on volunteers, it also increases the amount of activities available for people to plug into. Because volunteers don't need any long-term kind of religious education or high-up position in the church to start a program or help lead and teach others, lots of people with ideas for stuff come forward to try out their ideas. Not every idea gets turned into a class or an event, but the number of ideas keeps things fresh. New opportunities are always popping up. And by knowing their church has an open-door policy on church members suggesting things or getting involved, the overall church environment feels really inclusive. People can be as into things as they want to be without feeling like barriers or levels are blocking the way to participate.

3. TOUCH AND HEALING

If a church uses touch and healing, expect to be involved because individual spiritual energy is at the core of this kind of service. It's based on person-to-person contact and on the gifts of the Spirit each Christian receives, so it's the kind of thing you'd experience at services where people lay hands on one another, or get into worship by feeling free to clap, shout, dance, or do whatever as they feel moved by the Spirit.

Using touch and healing is powerful for two main reasons:

First, it brings the Spirit into clear view. A service that uses touch and healing makes the role of the Spirit plain. Because we've each got spiritual gifts that play a role in our lives and directly affect us, we can use these gifts to connect with God.

Second, services that use touch and healing give Christians a certain kind of emotional freedom that's not available at all churches. The whole range of emotions people feel during worship, or just in relation to life and to God in general, can be put right out there. And healing becomes really personalized. Members support one another. In times of sickness they help by gathering around, passing along their spiritual energy, and encouraging healing. Sometimes this leads to miracles, surges of spiritual power, or just all-around good feelings of being totally caught up in God's energy.

4. CONSISTENCY

When a church does its worship services based on any kind of specific time factor, what's going on is an attempt at consistency. Services that are consistent offer Christians a kind of guarantee. When you show up, the church service will be exactly this or that length and will be divided into sections that take a specific amount of time. For example, every service will start with a couple of minutes of silent prayer, then have five or six songs, then go on to the sermon, wrap up with some announcements, and then be all done. It'll all wrap up in about an hour and a half, and will always be divided into parts that last the same amount of time.

A consistent service makes it obvious right up front how much time you'll need to spend at church. So because it's about the quality of the time you spend connecting to God, not the length, a consistent service is one you can count on to fit in your busy schedule.

DIFFERENT SERVICES, ONE CONNECTION TO GOD

This quiz will help you find new ways to make your connection to God even stronger.

Churches do and use different things in worship services to enhance people's connection with God. So read the questions below and choose the answers that are most you, or most like something you'd like to try doing. At the end of the quiz you can check out what all your answers mean.

1. Some good spiritual growth might be on deck if I . . .

A Was baptized in a river or someplace I felt God's presence in a strong way.

B Learned enough that I could help perform really elaborate rituals.

C Started outwardly expressing more of the emotions I feel toward God.

D Used my faith to stand up against stuff like social injustice or war.

2. At church, it's easier for me to feel comfortable if . . .

A There aren't rules or divisions between who can and can't touch things or help out with services.

B Volunteers helping with the service know how everything should go and follow the lead of church leaders.

C I don't have to worry that the service will be a quiet, no-talking atmosphere.

D I know my church leaders have all gone to college and seminary.

3. How much should a worship service stick to a structured or formal plan?

A Plans are important, but you want them to be fun and not turn people off or be too confusing for people to follow.

B If you stick to a formal service, everybody knows what to expect and stuff feels more historic, even if it takes a little time to get the hang of it.

C You can't really plan what'll happen when God speaks through people, so it's better if the service is more relaxed, like something social that Christians are doing together.

D Planned readings and a calendar keep things consistent and give you the ability to read and apply biblical truths to new generations.

4. Would you rather stay more in the background with worship, letting art or ritual take center stage, or would you rather worship at a church where you could be more up front and get involved in the service and the way it goes?

A Staying back is good once in a while, but for the most part I like being more involved with the service.

B I'd rather do the background thing because there's already so much set up and going according to plan at the service.

C I don't have to be center stage, but I think it's better if people are all really active and can have a voice during the service.

D I like staying in the background at the service but want to know it can be updated as people's needs change.

5. Paying attention is no problem at church as long as the worship service . . .

A Is broken up into smaller chunks.

B Follows some kind of plan.

C Has some kind of way I can interact.

D Is related to what's going on in the world.

ANSWERS

If you picked mostly **A** answers, church services that use and do things based on being inclusive will give you a strong connection to God. These are services that give anybody who chooses an equal chance to participate and get involved. Any church group in the **ROSE**-colored section in Part Two of the book will offer connections like this.

If you picked mostly **B** answers, church services that use and do things based on things that tie you into the Christian picture as it has looked over time will give you a strong connection to God. These are run by people who know what's going on and how to make things consistent. Churches that set up connections with God this way are all in the **TEAL**-colored section in Part Two.

If you picked mostly **C** answers, services that use and do things based on hands-on worship and making sure everyone is able to express what they're feeling will give you a strong connection to God. These are services that keep things fresh by staying open to new expressions of the Spirit as it moves through people, and you can find that at any church in the **BLUE**-colored section in Part Two.

If you picked mostly **D** answers, church services that use and do things that make Christian traditions more flexible will give you a strong connection with God. These are services that emphasize the way your faith can impact the world to better things. Churches in the **PURPLE**-colored section in Part Two of the book are set up to run this way.

Taking God to the Streets

Religion and life can sometimes seem like two different things. It's not that we don't live out our faith, but it's that religion can get stuck in its own box while regular life gets stuck in another. And that's one of the main problems most Christians face: How do you get religion and life into the same box, instead of thinking of each separately?

One way to answer this question is to think about the apostles. They tied faith and life together by working as evangelists. After the death of Jesus, you could say the apostles basically became the street team for His teaching by spreading the Word, talking about Jesus and His miracles, and wandering off in different directions to preach and set up churches. And as time went on, a lot of other people followed in their footsteps. Ordinary people preached about Jesus to their friends, family, and neighbors while church leaders put the Word out in a bigger way through sermons that kept the evangelism thing on the front burner. For all these people, their lives and faith were tied together, as each kind of person did what they could to make Jesus' message known.

Over time, the kind of evangelism people were doing kept changing, but it still made a big impact and took the message of Christ to new places. To see what I mean, take a look at the history.

HOW EVANGELISM GOT FROM THERE TO HERE

1 Jesus makes waves with His interpretations of the Jewish Scriptures and His revolutionary claims about our purpose here on earth, our relationship to God, and what we can expect to inherit as God's children. Then the apostles take up where Jesus leaves off after His death and resurrection, basically kicking off street evangelism where people wander in different directions preaching the Good News.

2 Saul becomes Paul, being converted to Christianity when God decides to step in and have a word. Paul follows up on the work of the original apostles, but goes a step further by founding newbie church communities in various places as he zigzags across the Mediterranean and the Middle East so many times we need a ton of maps in the back of our Bibles just to keep track of all the places Paul went.

3 After Paul, in the third and fourth centuries (the 200s and 300s), a bunch of guys you've totally never heard of go places you probably didn't know any Christians went. For example, we've got our good buddy Pantænus preaching in India. And who could ever forget everyone's favorite fourth-century evangelist, Frumentius. The guy is a legend.

6 In 1663, the very first American Bible is printed. It's perfect . . . if you speak Algonquin, a Native American language. The first American Bible printing is made for evangelism, not for English-speaking Christians who already have Bibles of their own brought over from places like England.

5 Over the next five hundred years or so—across Europe and also in the Americas—sharing the message of Christ gets tied up with wars, conquests, and invasions. Many of the conversions Christians push for over these years end up becoming better known for their aggression than for their love.

4 Later, by the eleventh century (the 1000s), evangelism efforts have gone so far and so wide that the message of Christ is in remote places like Greenland, courtesy of one "Leif the Lucky." Or, as he's better known by his completely-less-fun-non-nickname name, Leif Ericson.

7 Straight-up preaching becomes the craze in evangelism after the 1700s. A guy named Jonathan Edwards begins a time in history known as the Great Awakening, and preaching tours are born. Festivals like today's Cornerstone music events are a modification of the kind of evangelism started during this time.

8 The 1900s bring a lot of individual Christians together to form bigger, better-established evangelism groups. The Christian & Missionary Alliance starts just about this time, and so does the Evangelical Alliance Mission (T.E.A.M.), Inter-Varsity, and later in this same century, Campus Crusade for Christ.

9 So here we are today, in the twenty-first century. Evangelism is still done using the street-team thing, but has become so much bigger than that too. Beyond even modern evangelism tools like the web, there are fusion efforts like prayer raves in Thailand or extreme sports demos featuring Christian bands.

Evangelism isn't the only way to keep religion and life tied together. Another way is to set up your life as an exact example of your beliefs. That means everything in your life reinforces your faith, so you're always trying to stay faithful in the face of constant compromise. You'd live in a place that didn't distract you from staying in touch with God on a regular basis. You'd have a job that promoted Christian values. Your friends would be people looking to glorify God in their personal relationships, and you'd be into hobbies that reflect the kind of morals, love, and charity that are at the core of Christian belief.

Basically, you'd live a life many people would consider weird since the whole deal would be about intentionally ditching things other people take for granted or do all the time. The lives of the apostles were like this. They lived together, stayed at the homes of other Christians when they traveled, and started up small communities where people tried to make the way they lived a cooperative, group deal. Lives that are set up in this way take God to the streets, not because they spread His Word in a verbal way, but because they reflect His truth. It's like a living illustration of all Jesus talks about, which means that people who see your lifestyle also see what's up with Christianity.

Evangelism or setting up your life as an example are two ways to tie religion together with your day-today living. If you go the evangelism route, you're doing exactly what Jesus asked. After He'd been resurrected, Jesus told people it was their job to share the Gospel so others could believe. And it's not like He was casual about it, being all, "Hey guys, if you get a sec would you go to that one province I missed over there?" Jesus wasn't asking believers to do Him a favor. He asked them to live out what they claimed to believe by spreading it on to others.

You can also do exactly what Jesus asked by going the life-as-an-example route. Almost every word in the Bible that Jesus said encourages believers to rid themselves of anything blocking their connection to spiritual growth. This means getting rid of the superficial gunk creating a barrier to seeing God clearly. It also means getting rid of the emotions (like greed, jealousy, or selfishness) that are holding you back from spiritual growth. Intentionally setting up a lifestyle to help filter these things out betters your chances of living your life as an example of what Jesus was saying.

When it comes down to it, the main deal is that you want religion and life to be united. But be realistic. Bringing faith and life together should be practical and work in a way that doesn't compromise your beliefs or blur the lines of what you're trying to do. Your church community is a place to get support.

How have you lived out your faith this month?

There you'll find other people trying to do the same thing, so you guys can all work together on breaking down the separate boxes between faith and life.

Just ask yourself what options are open around you to get God's Word out, and go for something straightforward. It's a long process to become a Christian who's mature enough to tie faith and life together on a regular basis. So you want to go with ideas that are solid and have clear goals you can watch yourself achieve. That'll make it easy to keep on track when times get hard or you feel like giving up.

Spiritual growth equals effort.

FAITH AND LIFE IN THE SAME COZY BOX

This quiz will help you see what kinds of things you're willing to do to tie faith and life together.

Evangelism is our job as Christians. Living life as an example is too. One or the other or some kind of mix of these two things will break down the separate boxes between life and faith.

Answer the questions below, then check out what your answers mean at the end of the quiz.

1. The easiest way to get people interested in Christianity is . . .

A To show them how easy Jesus makes it for us to be born again.

B To offer them something they need, like food, clothes, or a job.

C To show them a miracle or something powerfully life-changing.

D To be open to reinterpreting the message of Christ in all ages.

2. The all-time greatest evangelists are people like . . .

A Billy Graham, or stadium preachers like Harvest Crusade's Greg Laurie.

B Mother Teresa.

C Oral Roberts, Vineyard founder John Wimber, or Azusa Street Revival preacher William Seymour.

D People who fought for religious equality like Richard Allen or George Fox.

3. Evangelism isn't anything scary as long as . . .

A I can evangelize anywhere I think God is calling, not just one certain place I'm assigned to be.

B I can talk to people about faith but not have to host some kind of show or performance to reach a lot of people all at once.

C I can evangelize alongside other Christians who share my same core beliefs so we can focus on spreading the Word, not on the differences between us.

D I can do something other than witness about the gospel message, like put it into action instead.

4. If you want to reach the most people when you start a new church, it's important for things to be . . .

A   Set up by missionaries at a local church who want to start a sister church somewhere else.

B   Opened because the church government wants to establish more local church communities.

C   Not set up until people go to training or planning sessions.

D   Based on tradition and then shaped by the church's members.

5. Living life as an example of Jesus' message is most obvious to others when . . .

A   Christians keep reaching and converting others over time.

B   People know they can come to the church for help.

C   People see the Holy Spirit working in the life of a Christian.

D   Churches welcome and accept people as they are.

ANSWERS

If you picked mostly **A** answers, faith and life can come together in a clear way if you use stories, sermons, events, or preaching to get the Word of God out to the biggest number of people.

If you picked mostly **B** answers, faith and life can come together in a clear way if you make sure people see Christ's characteristics in the church and tell people about this symbolism.

If you picked mostly **C** answers, faith and life can come together in a clear way if you get the Word of God out to others by showing the results of what it can do in a person's life.

If you picked mostly **D** answers, faith and life can come together in a clear way if you learn more about places where you can effect change in the world by applying Christian values and modeling your lifestyle to others.

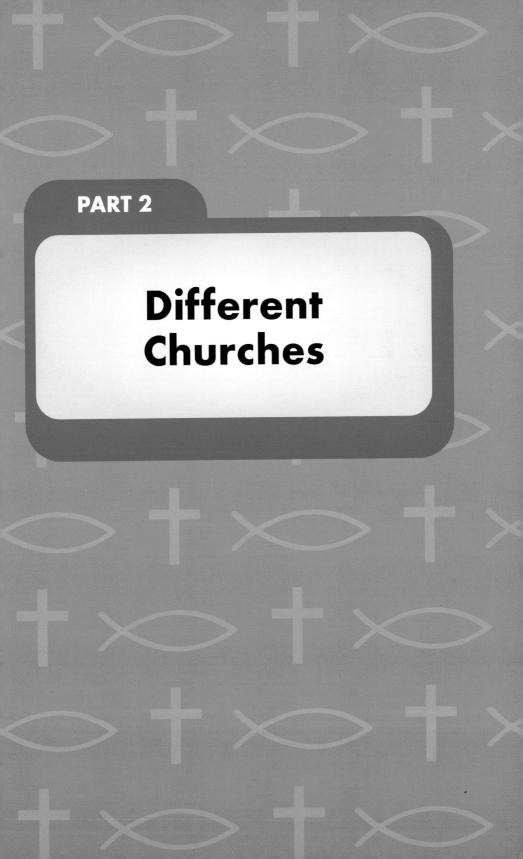

PART 2

Different Churches

EVANGELICAL and CONSERVATIVE

BIBLE CHURCHES

THE SHORT LIST

WHAT'S THE 1-2-3 RANK FOR THINGS TO FOCUS ON?

- Scripture
- Personal experience
- The traditions of fundamentalist Christianity

WHAT'S THE BIBLE?

- The final authority for Christians living in any age

WHAT'S THE CHURCH LIKE?

- Independent. There's no big central organization that runs all of the churches.

WHOM DO I CONTACT?

- No central organization or office. Check your local phone book.

When did this kind of Christianity get started?

Bible churches are independent communities that get started when Christians want to set up a church but don't want to join any kind of group or denomination that's already up and running. Bible churches are all about bypassing the synods, groups, assemblies, general conferences, and overall bigger structures that a lot of other kinds of Christianity use to organize things. There's also not a single, ultimate guy in charge, or a single book of worship or prayer, or any official sets of rules or doctrines Bible church Christians have to follow.

The idea to set up independent churches goes back to England. So imagine it's the 1800s and you're this guy named John Nelson Darby, and you're into God but you're not into picking and choosing between all the different kinds of Christianity. You don't really want to support the idea of a church that's set up as a kind of ministate or minigovernment, with councils and committees and laws and leaders and an overall church structure that puts leaders at the top and laypeople at the bottom. Darby just wants to worship God as a Christian. Not a particular kind of Christian, like an Anglican Christian, or a Catholic Christian, or a Presbyterian Christian.

What Darby did about his dilemma was to encourage people to focus on the Bible and set up churches where Scripture came first—not church government or any kind of favoritism for a particular kind of Christianity. When Darby hit the States, his ideas received backing from D. L. Moody, a guy with big pull in the Christian scene in Chicago at the time. A group of Christians working together at that time to rally around a set of statements called *The Fundamentals* picked up on Darby's ideas. These Christians were known as Fundamentalists, and it was with them that Darby's ideas became most popular.

Bible churches today are based on these roots. The churches are conservative or fundamentalist for the most part, and centered on Scripture. The biblical focus leads to a lot of evangelism, preaching, teaching, and helping others convert, in part because Moody was a big believer in millennialism (the belief that a thousand-year reign of peace is part of the future) and the end times and the Last Judgment.

Have I heard of them before?

Could be. Especially if you live in the suburbs or in some kind of place where housing is just being built or a lot of people have been moving in recently, you'll see Bible churches rolling into the neighborhood. Because these kinds of communities are independent, they're easy to get going and the focus on Scripture attracts a lot of people.

What makes this kind of Christianity unique?

- Pastors don't have to be formally trained for the job or have any kind of special degree.
- Though Bible churches have conservative beliefs for the most part, worship can be really modern. Some have punk bands, meditation classes, or amphitheater-style sanctuaries with plasma TVs.
- Each church gets by on just the donations of its members.
- Evangelism is a big deal at almost all Bible churches.

Is there a statement of faith (SOF)?

You can't really say there's one SOF every Bible church uses, but most share a lot of the same perspectives. A Bible church SOF will probably read a lot like this example: http://www.dentonbible.org/Welcome/doctrine.html.

Following are some of the main ideas and Bible verses a Bible church community might focus on:

- There will be a second coming when Christ returns to the earth, His judgment is laid down, and evil is stamped out: 1 Thessalonians 4:13–18, Philippians 3:20, Revelation 20:1–6.
- Christians need a kingdom mind-set. God has a purpose for each of us, and our lives should make the maximum possible impact for Christ.
- Answers for life and eternity are found in a personal relationship with Jesus Christ: Matthew 28:18–20, 1 Corinthians 9:19–23.

Who's in charge?

Each Bible church is its own deal and takes care of itself, because there is no larger group of churches to which it belongs. Pastors run the church and then each community decides on the other leadership positions they want to have, like deacons or elders.

What's the word for people my age?

Since each Bible church community is its own deal, what you'll find just depends on who runs things for people your age. This Bible church in Santa Cruz, California, gives you a good example of what kinds of things can turn up for people your age in a Bible church community: http://www.santacruzbible.org/youth/index.html.

Is there anything going on besides church?

Missions and evangelization are the main priorities for many Bible churches. Programs to spread God's Word sometimes go abroad, like this church's trips to Romania, Mexico, Africa, and beyond:
http://www.bearcreekbiblechurch.org/missions.shtml. Other evangelization opportunities stay local and get creative like this church is doing:
http://www.pbc.org/old-pbc1/missions/opportunities/. Lots of Bible churches have members who do the homeschooling thing. Churches also sometimes expand their campuses to include preschools, kindergartens, and even high schools. Usually, though, church school is something for the younger kids—but the overall point is to tie faith into all parts of a person's life, starting when they're really young. For an example, go to the website:
http://www.desertsprings.com/prek/index.html.

How can I hook up with this kind of Christianity?

The main way to find out about Bible churches is to give the web a go. Google "Bible churches" plus the name of your city or state. Scroll through what comes up and then spend some time visiting a few websites.

CHURCHES OF CHRIST

THE SHORT LIST

WHAT'S THE 1-2-3 RANK FOR THINGS TO FOCUS ON?

- Scripture
- Personal experience
- The traditions of restorationist Christianity

WHAT'S THE BIBLE?

- The authorative guide for faith and practice, in particular the texts of the New Testament

WHAT'S THE CHURCH LIKE?

- Independent. There's no big central organization that runs all of the churches.

WHOM DO I CONTACT?

- No central organization or office. Check your local phone book. Some addresses are listed on the following website: http://www.church-of-christ.org/.

When did this kind of Christianity get started?

The Churches of Christ were part of a bigger movement in American history called Restorationism (rest-oar-a-shun-is-um). The people in this movement were tired of all the versions of Christianity floating around and wanted to get things back to basics. They hoped to read the New Testament, see what the early church looked like, and copy what they saw. Just strict Bible truth. Nothing fancy or extra on the side.

During the 1800s, this idea caught on. The movement gained ground, pulling in almost a million members at a time when most people in America lived in just a few states on the East Coast and when Chicago wasn't even a city yet! Without a doubt, the Restoration Movement was one of the hottest things going. It spread fast, and a lot of the credit goes to early leaders of the Restoration Movement, like Alexander Campbell. Campbell was a guy who'd been raised in the Presbyterian Church and did the Baptist thing for a while, but eventually went his own way because he didn't want to be part of a church that caused divisions among believers. It was all about coming together as one set of Christians who all took the New Testament church as their guide.

For a while, things were good. The Restoration Movement had lots of members, and people kept focused on copying the early church of the Bible. But eventually the movement ran into trouble.

Just like any group with lots of people, some wanted to do things this way; others wanted to do things that way. People began to get into it over who was right, and eventually the Restoration Movement broke apart.

Some groups wanted to be more liberal and open to new ideas. The liberal groups wanted to read the Bible in a new way and expand what they believed in. Other groups said, "Um . . . how 'bout no!?" to this idea. They wanted to keep things the way they were—strict, plain, and simple. One of the groups that believed in keeping things the way they were eventually became known as the Churches of Christ.

Today, for the most part, the Churches of Christ stay out of disagreements between other kinds of churches and don't take sides when it comes to who's right or who's wrong. They just run their own communities according to what's written in the New Testament and hope all churches someday will do this too.

Have I heard of them before?

Probably so. If you live in the South or Southwest, you're kind of in the Churches of Christ epicenter. So, you probably have a friend who's a Church of Christ member or you've heard something about this kind of Christianity. If you live elsewhere, you may not have heard about it.

What makes this kind of Christianity unique?

- Churches of Christ try to set up local churches so they mirror many parts of the New Testament communities.
- Many Churches of Christ do not use instrumental music in their worship services because they believe the New Testament churches did not use instrumental music.
- There's usually no frou-frou architecture, decorations, or stained glass at a Church of Christ. Everything is stripped-down and way simple.
- Churches of Christ keep a close eye on the influence of Satan and the false teachings of the world.
- Churches of Christ are about Christian unity. The Christian Church shouldn't be split into lots of different groups.

Is there a statement of faith (SOF)?

Yes and no. Since each church is its own deal, you can't really say there's one SOF everybody is using. But Church of Christ communities are similar. They share a common purpose and set of beliefs along the lines of this example: http://vaughnpark.com/AboutVP/aboutVP.html.

Following are some of the main ideas and Bible verses a Church of Christ community might focus on:

- Christ created one united church: John 17:20–23, Ephesians 4:3–4.
- Christians can know everything necessary for salvation through Christ's example and teachings: Colossians 1:15–29, Ephesians 1:22–23.
- It's all about love: Mark 12:29–31.
- Getting the Gospel out to the world is key: Matthew 28:19–20.
- Baptism is key, but you have to be old enough to be able to express a desire for it, so no infant baptism.

Who's in charge?

The Churches of Christ are into following the example of the very first Christians. The type of leaders that you read about in the New Testament are the same type of leaders who run each Church of Christ community.

Elders hire the preacher with general approval of the congregation. Each Church of Christ is run independently, so each church sets its own qualifications for preachers. Preachers may have a degree in Bible or religious studies from a college or university, or have studied at a preacher training school.

What's the word for people my age?

Since each Church of Christ community is its own deal, what you'll find just depends on who runs things for people your age.

But one cool thing about the Churches of Christ is how international they are. Because there are so many members across the globe, you don't have to worry that you won't be able to find people your age. An international directory lets you meet people and keep in touch through a pen pal service online: http://church-of-christ.org/teens/bulletin-board/Pen-Pals.html.

Is there anything going on besides church?

Yep. The Churches of Christ publish magazines, books, and newspapers. They also serve the world through outreach programs and run schools and colleges all across America. Following are links for both things:

- The Christian Chronicle: http://www.christianity.com/christianchronicle
- The Gospel Advocate: http://www.gospeladvocate.com/gamagbod.htm
- New Wineskins: http://www.wineskins.org/
- Healing Hands International: http://www.hhi-aid.org/

If you're thinking it might be great to head to a Christian college, Churches of Christ beliefs are at the core of a bunch of colleges. Check out these schools:

http://www.mesachurch.org/web_links.htm#Universities

How can I hook up with this kind of Christianity?

The main way to find out about the Churches of Christ before you head off to visit a local church community is to do two things:

First, read a quick overview about this kind of Christianity at:

http://religiousmovements.lib.virginia.edu/nrms/restor2.html

Second, check out the Churches of Christ worldwide directory:

http://church-of-christ.org/churches/.

EMERGENT CHURCHES

THE SHORT LIST

WHAT'S THE 1-2-3 RANK FOR THINGS TO FOCUS ON?

- New approaches to worship
- Scripture
- Personal experience

WHAT'S THE BIBLE?

- A book inspired by God and the core foundation for Christian living

WHAT'S THE CHURCH LIKE?

- Independent. There's no big central organization that runs all of the churches, but many Emergent churches are small spinoff groups sponsored and supported by larger churches in the area.

WHOM DO I CONTACT?

- No central organization or office. Check the web or your local phone book for local Emergent churches.

When did this kind of Christianity get started?

Emergent churches are basically getting started all over the place right now, even as you read this sentence. It's that fresh of a thing. Emergent Christianity is Protestant, which means Emergent believers understand a person's relationship to God in a way that goes back to the Middle Ages and to a Catholic monk named Martin Luther. He encouraged Christians to believe in and follow nothing more and nothing less than what was written in the Bible, but he didn't think this was going on in Catholic Christianity. So by the time Luther laid out all his interpretations and ideas, it added up to a different kind of Christianity than Catholicism all together. Today we know Luther's ideas as Protestant Christianity. Emergent churches come up from this history.

So Emergent-style churches are new. That you know. But where did they come from? Well, the whole Emergent thing can kind of be looked at as a wave that followed megachurches. Sometimes this wave goes by another name: the postmodern church. In the end though, it's basically the same deal. It's all about reacting to what's come before in Christianity and saying, "Nah . . . we want something different, deeper, more creative, and more inclusive." And that makes the Emergent Movement a lot like most kinds of Christianity—it's a reaction to the past in the hope of redefining the way people relate to God.

Across the board, almost all Emergent churches want to move away from the slicked-out structure and intentional planning and general glossy "this-is-how-you-do-everything" Christianity promoted by megachurches and other large-scale Christian groups or denominations. Emergent churches are more interested in the journey of faith than the structure of it. But the overall Emergent Movement does revolve around a few key figures, the most high-profile guy being Pastor Brian McLaren. He basically sits at the Emergent epicenter. He's made a name for himself among younger generations of Christians, teaching them how to approach spirituality in ways that are creative and include all kinds of Christians. Also, McLaren urges Christians to consider religion something alive that interacts with modern culture while staying true to its roots and giving big ups to the built-in beauty of the historic Christian faith.

On the stability and longevity front, the future of Emergent Christianity is yet to be seen. Most Emergent communities have been run or started by people in their twenties and thirties, so it's still anybody's guess what'll happen to Emergent Christianity as these people age and Emergent churches grow. But since about the late 1990s, Emergent ideas have been popular and well received. Lots of Christians are getting involved, and it's generally seen as a fresh approach to Christianity for a modern world like ours.

Have I heard of them before?

It depends. You could have come across books by some of the people contributing a lot of ideas to the Emergent scene, like Pastor McLaren. Or you just might be in the right circles agewise to know a few people doing the Emergent thing, since it's mostly a college, twenties, and thirties thing at this point. And then you may know what's up with Emergent Christianity if you go to a big church, since a lot of Emergent groups are branch-offs from large church sponsors—because larger, more established churches sometimes branch out their ministries by founding and quietly funding Emergent communities. Many Emergent church leaders are those who are working for or with larger, more established churches that are sponsoring them.

What makes this kind of Christianity unique?

- Emergent churches put a priority on getting into discussion, worship, and fellowship with other kinds of Christian believers.
- Emergent churches think of themselves as free-form, creative places. Some do a lot of arts ministry, others focus on rituals, but all try to let individual creativity take the focus away from tightly planned and structured worship.
- Emergent churches don't have to stick to the same exact set of beliefs, so the overall movement has got more- and less-conservative groups all hanging together, each teaching a little bit different stuff in their church communities.

Is there a statement of faith (SOF)?

Local churches doing the Emergent thing usually do have a list of beliefs, sometimes based on historical confessions of Christianity like the Nicene Creed or the Apostles' Creed. But overall it's a no-go on official statements of faith that define Emergent Christianity. One of the main points of the movement is that you don't have to make everything so official or structured.

Following are some of the main ideas an Emergent church community might focus on:

- Church should be a welcoming, dynamic place. Judgment and stuffy services are out.
- Christian faith is an ongoing story that's written by your own walk with God. Connecting to the divine and growing spiritually are key.
- Worship and church life should be as creative and expressive as the people in any church community, not preplanned and packaged.
- God's Word is supposed to get out to others. Christians are to promote His message as lovingly as they can.

Who's in charge?

Start a church; you're in charge. Emergent churches aren't a formal or big official organization, so there's nobody running the whole show.

Each local church does its own thing, makes up its own rules, manages its own money, and decides on the spiritual path that's best in terms of overall Emergent-style goals.

What's the word for people my age?

Since each Emergent community is its own deal, what you'll find just depends on who runs things for people your age.

On a national level, though, you've got conferences like Emergent YS, which is all about deepening the Emergent conversation. Check into the next conference online: http://www.emergentconvention.com/.

Is there anything going on besides church?

Local Emergent communities do focus on evangelism, and Emergent Christians are especially good at reaching out to those who do not attend church. In a more overall sense, books, conferences, blogs, and websites are the main deal for Emergent churches because most things going on in the wider Emergent Movement are focused on getting Emergent beliefs, ideas, and values out on a bigger scale. Following is an online list of blogs where Emergent leaders talk about what's going on, what's next, and where the movement should go: http://www.vintagefaith.com/links.html#blogs.

How can I hook up with this kind of Christianity?

Reading and virtual visiting are the best ways to hook up with the Emergent crowd.

To read, snag a book by any of these authors: Brian McLaren, Dan Kimball, Leonard Sweet, Tony Jones, or Spencer Burke. Or go online for a seriously huge resource list of more Emergent stuff than you'll find anywhere else: http://www.agts.edu/faculty/faculty_publications/bibliographies/creps_bibliography/index.html.

To do the virtual visit thing, visit the web and get a sense of what Emergent churches are all about from these example communities:

- Scum of the Earth: http://www.scumoftheearth.net
- Blue Sky Church: http://www.blueskychurch.com
- Apex: http://www.apexchurch.org

EVANGELICAL LUTHERAN CHURCH IN AMERICA

THE SHORT LIST

WHAT'S THE 1-2-3 RANK FOR THINGS TO FOCUS ON?

- Scripture
- The traditions of Lutheran Christianity
- The personal experience you get from the sacraments (rituals)

WHAT'S THE BIBLE?

- The primary place Christians look to form their beliefs, even if all Christians don't always come to the same conclusions when interpreting God's Word

WHAT'S THE CHURCH LIKE?

- Teamed up with others. Churches cooperate with one another, sending members and leaders to an assembly that decides things for everybody.

WHOM DO I CONTACT?

- 8765 W. Higgins Rd., Chicago, IL 60631
- Phone: (800) 638-3522; Fax (773) 380-1465
- URL: http://www.elca.org/

When did this kind of Christianity get started?

Lutheran Christianity ties itself back to the Middle Ages and the German monk Martin Luther, who nailed up the main ideas he thought were central to the Christian faith, helping to get the Protestant Christian movement started. His ideas didn't jump from Europe in the Middle Ages straight to America, though. Obviously, it took years for Luther's kind of Christianity to make its way to the States.

First, it had to get picked up and preached all over places like Germany, Norway, Sweden, Denmark, Iceland, and Finland.

Second, it had to get passed down over time, and then finally when Christians from these areas of Europe made their way to America as immigrants, they brought Lutheran Christianity with them.

Early on, the different Lutheran Christians in America supported one another. But like lots of Christian groups, Lutherans ended up splitting up. Most of them landed in one of two camps, one of them being the Evangelical Lutheran Church of America (ELCA). (Check out the profile in this section for the Lutheran Church–Missouri Synod to read more about the other major group of Lutheran Christians.) So the ELCA group got its official start in the 1980s and has been growing since that time. Today it's one of the biggest groups of Protestant churches in America.

Have I heard of them before?

Maybe. The ELCA might not be a specific group you've heard of, but Martin Luther is a name you might recognize. If no place else, you run into his name in history books—since Luther basically started the whole Middle Ages movement known as the Reformation.

What makes this kind of Christianity unique?

- ELCA churches ordain women as pastors.
- The Bible is not used as a literal record of stuff that actually happened on a historical level.
- ELCA Christians follow a yearly calendar for Bible readings like Catholic and Orthodox Christians, but they don't do as many rituals.

Is there a statement of faith (SOF)?

The Constitution of the Evangelical Lutheran Church in America is the statement ELCA churches stick to. It's online at: http://www.elca.org/secretary/Constitutions/ConstitutionsIntro.html.

Following are some of the main ideas and Bible verses an ELCA community might focus on:

- Prayer deepens spiritual maturity and is also a way to reach out to others: Matthew 26:40, Psalm 147:1.
- Lutheran Christianity is designed to be plain and easy to understand. Three phrases sum up what's essential:
    1. Grace alone
    2. Faith alone
    3. Scripture alone
- Christians are united by faith no matter what church they belong to and should get together since we've all been restored by God to Christ: Acts 2.
- Communion is a way to fellowship as a family. It symbolizes the joy Christians all share in Jesus' resurrection: Isaiah 25:6, Acts 2:46.

Who's in charge?

A Churchwide Assembly is at the highest rung of the ELCA. It's the place where ELCA churches can send representatives to vote on different rules, policies, and so forth that'll end up getting followed at each local ELCA church.

At the local level a girl or a guy works as a minister, running everything and keeping the church centered on ELCA-style beliefs. Other leadership positions are left up to each local church.

What's the word for people my age?

The main ELCA website has a section just for youth ministry that's got a calendar so you can see what's up for the whole year: http://www.elca.org/dcm/youth/index.html.

You can also check out LYO, the Lutheran Youth Organization. It's a central hub-type deal that'll point you in the right direction, if you want to get more involved with ministries sponsored by the ELCA. That's at: http://www.elca.org/dcm/youth/lyo/.

Is there anything going on besides church?

The ELCA works with lots of different kinds of Christians so churches are always talking, meeting, and getting together through their Department for Ecumenical Affairs ministry: http://www.elca.org/ea/.

ELCA Christians talk, debate, and get into discussions about biblical interpretation and Christian beliefs. Being educated enough to have these kinds of discussions is something ELCA churches encourage so there are always articles, debates, and ideas put in magazines you can read online, like these two:

⊂⊃ *The Lutheran:* http://www.thelutheran.org/
⊂⊃ *Lutheran Partners:* http://www.elca.org/lp/

World ministry and local outreach efforts are also part of ELCA Christianity, and there's a central place for that online at: http://www.elca.org/resources.html.

If you're thinking it'd be great to head to a Christian college, ELCA beliefs are at the core of a bunch of colleges. Check out these schools: http://www.elca.org/colleges/college.html.

How can I hook up with this kind of Christianity?

The main way to find out about ELCA Christianity is to visit their main website and to use the church locator link to find a church near you if you like what you see: http://www.elca.org/index.html.

LUTHERAN CHURCH –MISSOURI SYNOD

THE SHORT LIST

WHAT'S THE 1-2-3 RANK FOR THINGS TO FOCUS ON?

- Scripture
- The traditions of Lutheran Christianity
- The personal experience you get from the sacraments (rituals)

WHAT'S THE BIBLE?

- The primary book Christians use to shape their beliefs, even if all Christians don't always agree about which beliefs are most important

WHAT'S THE CHURCH LIKE?

- Teamed up with others. Churches choose to cooperate with one another and keep the same values and beliefs.

WHOM DO I CONTACT?

- 1333 S. Kirkwood Rd., St. Louis, MO 63122-7295
- Phone: (888) 843-5267; Fax (314) 996-1016
- URL: http://www.lcms.org/

When did this kind of Christianity get started?

Not surprisingly, the Lutheran Church—Missouri Synod (LCMS) got up and running in Missouri. Of course, it's not just a church for people in Missouri anymore. It's huge, and a lot of its appeal is based on the history that church has got tying itself back to Europe in the Middle Ages and to the religious Reformer Martin Luther. He's the German monk who broke from the Catholic Church and began to focus on new and different kinds of biblical interpretations that today we call Protestant Christianity.

Even though Lutheran Christianity didn't land in America until the nineteenth century (the 1800s), it spread across places in Europe for years and became a stable kind of Christianity with a strong following. The first Lutheran pastors to arrive in America were just a group of twelve guys from Germany, but they had the Lutheran connection to all that history. The guys kept connected to Lutheranism's solid foundation, and that attracted immigrants in America who had been Lutherans in their home countries.

So LCMS Christianity started out with those first twelve guys and groups of other believers who were mostly from Germany and new to America. Eventually, it reached beyond just Germans or just people with Lutheran backgrounds (or just people in Missouri!) and started pulling in all kinds of believers. With growth came division, and today the LCMS is considered the conservative branch of Lutheran Christianity, while other Lutheran groups (like a church that's profiled in this book, the Evangelical Lutheran Church of America) are more liberal. Despite their differences, Lutheranism still points back to the core points of Martin Luther's ideas and has enough followers to be a big slice of the American religious pie with a well-established history.

Have I heard of them before?

Maybe. LCMS Christianity might not be a specific kind of Christian faith you've heard of, but Martin Luther is a guy you may know. If no place else you might have run into his name in history books—since Luther basically started the whole Middle Ages movement known as the Reformation.

What makes this kind of Christianity unique?

- All the Lutheran churches in the Missouri Synod make an ongoing, active decision to belong to the group, rather than, say, a Roman Catholic church that's established and part of the church body because that's what's been decided by leaders higher up in the overall church government.
- Lutheran Christianity is designed to be plain and easy to understand. Three phrases sum up what's essential:
  1. Grace alone.
  2. Faith alone.
  3. Scripture alone.
- LCMS Christians use the Book of Concord, since it lays out what's believed, taught, and practiced at LCMS churches.

Is there a statement of faith (SOF)?

LCMS Christians place a huge amount of importance on the confessions collected in the *Book of Concord*. These confessions are really old and go back to the start of the faith—to Luther's own writings.

Following are some of the main ideas and Bible verses a LCMS community might focus on:

- In Communion, Jesus isn't symbolized. He's really there. He's present, but not in the same exact way as when Jesus was on earth.
- From the beginning of time God has planned to save us by His grace, and we contribute to His plan by preaching the Word to others: Romans 11:33–36, Ephesians 3:7–8, 1 Corinthians 9:16.
- The only standard for Christian belief and church function is the Word of God: 2 Timothy 3:16, 2 Peter 1:20–21.
- Seeking God's kingdom is about learning to participate fully in God's grace given to us in Christ: John 3:5, Matthew 6:33.

Who's in charge?

The Regular Convention is the main meeting where general rules, ideas, structures, and administrative stuff are taken care of for all the partner churches. And the president of the entire Missouri Synod is in charge of keeping things on track in terms of staying committed to Lutheran principles of Christianity.

At the local level, each LCMS church is its own deal and takes care of itself. Pastors head the church and then each church can decide on optional positions, like deacons or elders.

What's the word for people my age?

Since each LCMS community is its own deal, what you'll find just depends on who runs things for people your age. In general, you can keep up with LCMS youth stuff at thESource, a website shared by the partner churches: http://www.youthesource.com. Or you can check out this list of monthly events, collections of resources, and LCMS updates:
http://www.lcms.org/pages/internal.asp?NavID=1798.

Is there anything going on besides church?

The LCMS runs the Concordia Publishing House. It's unique in that it doesn't just do regular publishing stuff, but also puts out books in Braille for blind people and ministry resources for the hearing-impaired. You can check it out at: http://www.cph.org/.

If you're thinking it'd be great to head to a Christian college, LCMS beliefs are at the core of a bunch of colleges. Check out these schools: http://www.lcms.org/pages/default.asp?NavID=886.

How can I hook up with this kind of Christianity?

The main way to find out about LCMS Christianity is to visit their main website: http://www.lcms.org/.

MENNONITES
The Mennonite Church, USA

THE SHORT LIST

WHAT'S THE 1-2-3 RANK FOR THINGS TO FOCUS ON?

- Scripture
- Personal experience
- The traditions of Anabaptist / Mennonite Christianity

WHAT'S THE BIBLE?

- The Word of God and the final deal when it comes to trustworthy standards for Christian living

WHAT'S THE CHURCH LIKE?

- Teamed up with others. Churches choose to cooperate with one another and keep the same values and beliefs.

WHOM DO I CONTACT?

- P.O. Box 1245, Elkhart, IN 46515-1245
- Phone: (866) 866-2872
- URL: http://www.mennoniteusa.org/

When did this kind of Christianity get started?

Before Mennonites were Mennonites they were Anabaptists. That was the group's first name: Anabaptists, which means *re-baptizer*. See, the group wasn't satisfied with baptism being just another kind of Christian ritual. They wanted baptism to be out in the open, done on purpose, and work as a kind of sign that said, "I'm a Christian—right here, right now!" Baptism was a sign of personal faith for Anabaptists, so they began rebaptizing each other and those who joined the group, even if they'd already been baptized as infants or children.

So one day a guy named Menno Simons joined the Anabaptists who were living in Holland. He began to lead the group and emphasized scriptural points like Christian community, generosity, sharing, and turning the other cheek. All his ideas got so much support that Anabaptists eventually became known by the interpretations of Menno and were then called Mennonites. Some of these Christians eventually emigrated from Holland and settled down in Pennsylvania, bringing Mennonite Christianity to America.

In Pennsylvania Mennonites would gather and worship without taking flack for not being like other kinds of Christianity already set up at the time. And since Mennonite living was all about community, generosity, sharing, and turning the other cheek, people basically provided for one another, setting up a solid base for believers. Today things are pretty much the same. Mennonite groups aren't huge in number, but they work together and continue to attract members as the years go by.

Have I heard of them before?

Almost for sure. You've heard of Amish Christianity, right? Well, Amish Christians practice a very similar form of Christianity, started by a guy named Jacob Amman. The Amish live in closed, tight-knit communities, dress conservatively (we're talking bonnets here), and don't have stuff most people take for granted these days, like cars, phones, or computers.

Mennonites are more liberal than the Amish, staying aligned with the teachings about community, generosity, sharing, and turning the other cheek that Menno Simons focused on all those years back.

What makes this kind of Christianity unique?

- Mennonites support nonviolence and feel that war, racism, violence, abortion, and things like the death penalty are things Christians should witness against.
- A Mennonite's first allegiance is to God, who is Truth. So they don't swear oaths to guarantee anything, like oaths of allegiance. Instead, they believe Christians should tell the truth without oaths in everything from family life to other agreements people are required to make in life, like business deals.
- Mennonites worship God by serving Him through society and life. Working and living together as a community and using their resources for outreach ministries are a major focus in Mennonite communities.

Is there a statement of faith (SOF)?

Back when Mennonites were Anabaptists, they stood by something called the Schleitheim Articles, also known as the Schleitheim Confession. Okay, but that was in 1527. Things have been updated in terms of beliefs most Mennonites call their own, and now things center on the Confession of Faith in a Mennonite Perspective: http://www.mcusa-archives.org/library/resolutions/1995/index.html.

Following are some of the main ideas and Bible verses a Mennonite church might focus on:

- The church is more than just an organization. It's a community: Acts 2:42.
- Spiritual leaders for the church can be girls or guys since either could lead the kind of holy life that would make a great witness for God: Ephesians 4:11–13, Romans 12:6–8, 1 Timothy 3:1–13.
- Nonviolence is one of the highest Christian priorities and allows us to live out the teachings of Jesus: Matthew 5:39.

Who's in charge?

On the local level, Mennonite churches appoint their own pastors, elders, and other church officers.

At the top of Mennonite Christianity is the General Conference. It's made up of Mennonite representatives from different local churches that get together to decide on things like the general rules, ideas, structures, and administrative things everybody's going to follow.

What's the word for people my age?

Since each Mennonite community is its own deal, what you'll find just depends on who runs things for people your age.

Something held on Mennonite college campuses is the Y-LEAD conference: http://www.goshen.edu/ylead/. And then you can also find a directory that'll link you to regional Mennonite groups offering different stuff to get involved in: http://directory.mennoniteusa.org/conferences.asp.

Is there anything going on besides church?

The Mennonite Mission Network is cool since it's a media outlet that puts out all kinds of movies, CDs, and radio spots, and also runs a pretty sweet website with just about everything related to Mennonites in America and in Canada. Give it a look: http://www.thirdway.com/. Or head over to this link and get the full list of things the Mennonite Mission Network is involved in: http://www.mennonitemission.net/work/.

If you're thinking it'd be great to head to a Christian college, Mennonite Christianity is at the core of a bunch of schools: http://www.mennoniteeducation.org/MEAPortal/DesktopDefault.aspx?tabid=38.

How can I hook up with this kind of Christianity?

There are a few different big groups of Mennonites today, and you can read about each of them to see which you like best.

- Mennonite Church, U.S.A.: http://www.mennoniteusa.org/
- U.S. Conference of Mennonite Brethren Churches: http://www.usmb.org/index.cfm

If you want more of a summary about Mennonite Christianity in general, try:

http://religiousmovements.lib.virginia.edu/nrms/mennonites.html.

Also, give a look at the links listed for Amish Christianity. Remember, though, the Amish aren't doing the whole *www* thing. It's a no-tech zone in Amish communities, so the links below are *about* Amish Christians, not websites *run by* Amish Christians.

- About the Amish: http://religiousmovements.lib.virginia.edu/nrms/amish.html
- The Amish Country News: http://www.amishnews.com/

NONDENOMINATIONAL CHURCHES

THE SHORT LIST

WHAT'S THE 1-2-3 RANK FOR THINGS TO FOCUS ON?

- Scripture
- Personal experience
- The Christian tradition

WHAT'S THE BIBLE?

- A book inspired by God that Christians look to as their authority for living

WHAT'S THE CHURCH LIKE?

- Independent. There's no big central organization that runs all of the churches.

WHOM DO I CONTACT?

- No central organization or office. Check your local phone book.

When did this kind of Christianity get started?

In America, nondenominational churches weren't anything that took off as one big trend. It was more like independent churches sprang up here and there, each wanting to do things on its own without having to belong to any larger group. Individuals are at the core of nondenominational churches, so basically all you have to do to start a nondenominational church is start one. There's no church history you have to be a part of and no set of beliefs you have to agree with. That means nondenominational churches don't have an exact beginning in American history since each is and has always been its own deal. Still, a steady stream of these kinds of church communities showed up on a regular basis after about 1950. Each has been founded on scriptural beliefs, and the Bible remains the guiding force for direction and organization in these churches.

And that's about it. There's really no long history lesson here. Nondenominational churches are fairly new to the religious scene. Earlier kinds of Christianity obviously have longer histories in America, but that hasn't mattered in terms of how popular the nondenominational idea has been. No matter how you read the Bible or how many people show up at your services, you can start a nondenominational church.

Have I heard of them before?

Probably. Even if you haven't seen a church that says "nondenominational" in its title, there's a good chance you know someone who goes to a nondenominational community. They're really widespread, especially in places like new suburban areas that are expanding or having a lot of people move in.

What makes this kind of Christianity unique?

- Nondenominational churches don't look back to any person or group or idea for their history. A church's history starts when the church does.
- Most nondenominational churches preach conservative beliefs and stress evangelization. They reach out to "seekers" looking for a spiritual home.
- Nondenominational churches stress each person's individual relationship with Jesus. They want Christians to grow in Christ.
- Anyone called by God can start up a church, so it's not uncommon for a nondenominational church to start with just two or three members.

Is there a statement of faith (SOF)?

Since each nondenominational church decides on its own set of beliefs, the SOF is unique in each community. A good example of the kinds of things most nondenominational churches care about will look something like what's found on this website:
http://www.chandlercc.org/.

Following are some of the main ideas and Bible verses a nondenominational community might focus on:

- Everyone is a sinner separated from God until they accept Jesus as their Savior: Ephesians 2:8–9, Acts 4:12.
- Nondenominational Christianity is a fellowship of believers who have no creed but Christ, and no book but the Bible.
- The Lord's Supper (Communion) is a symbolic way to remember Jesus: 1 Corinthians 11:24–25, Matthew 26:26–29.
- Christ will return to earth and all Christians will be raised to eternal life: Acts 1:11, 1 Thessalonians 4:13–18.

Who's in charge?

Each local church is completely its own deal, so you'll have a pastor who leads the congregation, but then after that it's up to the church community how many other leadership positions they want to have. Some nondenominational churches use elders or deacons; some don't.

What's the word for people my age?

Since each nondenominational church is its own deal, what you'll find just depends on who runs things for people your age. Give this website a look as an example: http://www.buckheadchurch.org/students.

Is there anything going on besides church?

Evangelism and caring for the members of your own local church are at the core of most nondenominational communities.

In terms of evangelism, this is usually tied into the church through mission trips or missionaries working across the world to bring people to Christ.

In terms of outreach for church members there are various ministries that offer support and guidance to Christians, including youth, singles, divorce, and counseling ministries.

If you're thinking it might be great to head to a Christian college, nondenominational beliefs aren't at the core of any single bunch of colleges, but you'll probably be in your zone by checking into Protestant Christian colleges.

How can I hook up with this kind of Christianity?

The main way to find out about nondenominational churches is to give the Web a go. Google "nondenominational churches" plus the name of your city or state. Scroll through what comes up and then spend some time visiting a few websites.

SALVATION ARMY

THE SHORT LIST

WHAT'S THE 1-2-3 RANK FOR THINGS TO FOCUS ON?

- Scripture
- Personal experience
- The traditions of Salvation Army Christianity

WHAT'S THE BIBLE?

- A book inspired by God that's the main rule for Christian faith and practice

WHAT'S THE CHURCH LIKE?

- Controlled from the top down. Local churches run things according to what higher-up leaders say.

WHOM DO I CONTACT?

- P.O. Box 269, Alexandria, VA 22313
- Phone: (703) 684-5500
- URL: http://www1.salvationarmy.org/

When did this kind of Christianity get started?

Like a lot of kinds of Christianity in America, the Salvation Army started someplace else. In England, to be exact. Over there, Minister John Wesley's ideas about living by a set of particular ideas about prayer, fasting, Bible reading, and doing charitable works became known as Methodism, since they taught a kind of *method* for Christian living. John Booth was a guy these Methodist teachings appealed to, and though he worked as a Methodist leader for a while, he eventually focused on the charitable works part of the deal. Booth began to preach that a Christian life should be mostly focused on service and plopped his ministry efforts right in the middle of the poorest place in London. He wanted to get lots of different Christian groups to help out with his idea, but that didn't end up working out. So as Booth began to expand his social outreach ministry, he basically did most of the work himself. Eventually he generated a big enough following to start up a new kind of Christianity almost exclusively focused on serving the poor, meeting people's needs, and spreading the gospel message.

But again, all this was in England. Salvation Army Christianity didn't make its way to America until 1880. Booth's friend, a guy named George Scott Railton, was the first person to set up shop with Salvation Army Christianity. He did the same thing Booth did in England, setting up Salvation Army churches in the poorest parts of town and getting right down to the business of serving others. And his timing was great. The early 1900s were full of unemployed Americans, needy people, and poor immigrants, and overall there were a lot of people who needed a hand. So that's what the Salvation Army offered through food, housing, shelter, and job programs.

The Salvation Army became known for all this help, but social service wasn't the only reason this kind of Christianity had staying power. See, the Salvation Army isn't called an "army" for nothing. The basic idea is that Christians make up a kind of spiritual army. Everything in the Salvation Army reflects this. Churches are called "corps." Pastors are "officers" who hold different ranks. Higher-up church leaders also have military names, and then at the top you've got the general. In other kinds of Christianity this would be something like the president or general minister, but with the Salvation Army, everything is military-related. Salvation Army Christians (called "soldiers") even dressed military. They'd bust out uniforms that everyone could see and identify, and they still wear uniforms today sometimes.

The tightly controlled, highly organized military structure of the Salvation Army has made the group really successful. Even though it's a more recent kind of Christianity than some others, it's got a big following and is a global movement.

Have I heard of them before?

Almost for sure. You might have given away clothes and items to the Salvation Army, or at least passed the Salvation Army volunteer in red ringing a bell at Christmastime, asking people to throw change into the red bucket.

What makes this kind of Christianity unique?

- The Salvation Army is a combo deal: part charity organization, part church. It's not just one or the other.
- Everything in the Salvation Army is military, from the names you use for church leaders (like general or lieutenant) to the way you think about Christianity (Christians are at war with sin).
- Worldwide donations and revenue taken in by the Salvation Army pushes near the billion-dollar mark (yeah, "B" . . . Billion) almost every year. They're serious about social services and use these big-time funds to pay for it all.
- Salvation Army services don't do the Communion or baptism thing. These rituals aren't considered right or wrong; the Salvation Army just doesn't do them.

Is there a statement of faith (SOF)?

There's a statement of faith, but it's not called that. Keeping things military, the Salvation Army calls it the Soldier's Covenant (or the Articles of War): http://www1.salvationarmy.org/ihq/ www_sa.nsf/vw-dynamic-arrays/600EEABFF964EDFE 80256D58004B4D58?openDocument.

Following are some of the main ideas and Bible verses a Salvation Army community might focus on:

- Living for Jesus means incorporating prayer, study, witnessing, charity, and fellowship together in your life: Psalm 55:17, Romans 10:9, Luke 9:23.
- The motto "Heart to God and hand to man" is a good way to sum up Salvation Army Christianity.
- Salvation is an A-B-C plan: Admit your need. Believe in Christ. Commit yourself to Christ.

Who's in charge?

In short: the general. Salvation Army communities are under the administrative control of a single general who guides all Salvation Army groups.

As for the local level, that's where most of the charity work is getting done. Local Salvation Army groups work under the command of an officer and are then further divided into different divisions and territories depending on what part of the country a Salvation Army group is located in.

What's the word for people my age?

Since Salvation Army groups are divided into territories, you can link up with youth doing things in your part of the country:

- Eastern Territory: http://www1.salvationarmy.org/use%5Cwww_use.nsf/vw-sublinks/39EF801349BB415E85256F00006044C0?openDocument
- Central Territory: http://www.usc.salvationarmy.org/youth/camping.htm
- Western Territory: http://www1.salvationarmy.org/usw/www_usw.nsf/vw-dynamic-arrays/88256D3D006526AD88256BDE00015BA7?openDocument
- Southern Territory: http://www.youthdownsouth.org/

Is there anything going on besides church?

Social service, social service, social service. It's at the core of Salvation Army Christianity, so local groups basically do some of everything, and that's where you can plug into stuff going on.

Let's see . . . you could choose to volunteer by serving food to the hungry, caring for the poor, offering day care, running boys and girls clubs, operating medical centers, giving aid and shelter to disaster victims, running job-training programs, ministering to prisoners, doing the radio thing, evangelizing across the globe, supplying back-to-school essentials for needy kids, finding missing persons, or making doughnuts. Yeah, for real. The Salvation Army makes really good doughnuts. Check it out online: http://www.nwarmy.org/ourstory/history_doughnut.asp.

How can I hook up with this kind of Christianity?

The main way to find out about Salvation Army Christianity is to visit their main website:
http://www1.salvationarmy.org/ihq/www_sa.nsf.

Then you can link to their FAQ pages to learn more about specific Salvation Army ideas, because the group might be different from what you're used to, being that it's a church/charity-type deal rather than just a church:
http://www.salvationarmy.org.uk/en/Library/factSheets/Home.htm.

SOUTHERN BAPTIST
Southern Baptist Convention

THE SHORT LIST

WHAT'S THE 1-2-3 RANK FOR THINGS TO FOCUS ON?

- Scripture
- Personal experience
- The traditions of Baptist Christianity

WHAT'S THE BIBLE?

- A perfect treasure of divine instruction, authored by God and without error

WHAT'S THE CHURCH LIKE?

- Teamed up with others. Churches choose to cooperate with one another and keep the same values and beliefs.

WHOM DO I CONTACT?

- Office of Convention Relations
- 901 Commerce St., Nashville, TN 37203-3699
- Phone: (615) 244-2355
- URL: http://www.sbc.net/

When did this kind of Christianity get started?

In America, Baptist Christianity got rolling with the arrival of Christians from England. John Smyth and Thomas Helwys separated from the church they had been going to in order to focus on two things: to make central to their faith the idea that God's grace was something for everyone, and a belief in adult baptism. The baptism thing is where Baptist Christians get their name, since baptism is only for people old enough to understand it and choose it.

By the 1600s, Baptists had hit America's East Coast. Quickly they expanded Baptist Christianity down into the South and other places, but like lots of Christian groups, they ended up splitting into different groups. One of the big things dividing Baptists was slavery—some Baptists were in support of it, but others weren't. At the time, slavery wasn't an issue all Christians agreed was wrong—so the Baptists were caught on two sides just like many other Christian groups. Despite the split, Baptist beliefs stayed true to the core things Smyth and Helwys cared about. Adult baptism became the main thing people knew about Baptists.

By the start of the 1900s, certain Baptists came together to create the Southern Baptist Convention (SBC). They left things alone when it came to each local church, but set up associations between all the churches and set up boards to pair Baptists together so they could evangelize and do missions work more effectively. Since then, the SBC has become a strong, stable, and expanding part of modern Christianity with deep roots in American history.

Have I heard of them before?

Almost for sure. The SBC is H-U-G-E! More than 40,000 SBC churches dot America's landscape, and they're doing mission work in more than 150 nations worldwide.

What makes this kind of Christianity unique?

- Churches in the SBC choose to belong.
- Nothing makes you a Christian according to SBC Christianity except your belief in Jesus Christ. Not baptism, or church membership, or following a particular priest or pastor, or keeping up with regular rituals.
- Most SBC churches preach conservative beliefs, but you still get a little bit of a variation among local churches since they're each in charge of their own congregation.
- SBC churches practice adult baptism with total immersion, which means you've got to be old enough to make your own choice to be baptized and you've gotta get all the way dunked when it happens.

Is there a statement of faith (SOF)?

SBC churches use the Baptist Faith and Message: http://www.sbc.net/bfm/bfm2000.asp.

Following are some of the main ideas and Bible verses a SBC church community might focus on:

- Evangelism isn't just a duty. It's a privilege: Matthew 9:37–38, Ephesians 3:1–11, 2 Timothy 4:5.
- Husbands and wives are of equal worth, but God has given them different roles in life. God wants husbands to lead the family and wants wives to support their leadership: Ephesians 5:21–33, Colossians 3:18–21.
- Church and state should be separate, but it's the duty of Christians to support their government leaders as long as stuff doesn't go against the will of God: Acts 4:19–20, Romans 13:1–7.

Who's in charge?

Each SBC church is its own deal and takes care of itself, but there are standards of belief when it comes to being included, and churches participate in a convention of all the SBC churches to get direction for where they're all going as a group.

Pastors run things on a day-to-day basis, keep things in line with SBC values, and hook up with other SBC churches in the area. Only men hold the position of pastor.

What's the word for people my age?

Since each SBC church community is its own deal, what you'll find just depends on who runs things for people your age.

On a national level, one site combines links to everything from evangelization tools to info on retreats to places you can hook up with campus missions programs, get in touch with a counselor, or find new ways to grow spiritually. It's the SBC Youth Resource site: http://www.sbc.net/families/youthresources.asp.

Is there anything going on besides church?

Missions and evangelization are the main priorities of SBC Christianity. Boards are set up to take care of outreach in particular areas of the globe. To learn what's going on with each board, check out the following websites:

International Mission Board: http://www.imb.org/core/default.asp

American Missions: http://www.namb.net/site/pp.asp?c=9qKILUOzEpH&b=213008

The Cooperative Program: http://www.sbc.net/redirect.asp?url=http://www.cpmissions.net

Articles about faith and life are featured in the journal of the SBC, called *SBC Life,* which is online at: http://sbclife.net/. And then you can also read about world events and national news from a SBC perspective in *BPNews,* the SBC's newsmagazine: http://bpnews.net/.

If you're thinking it'd be great to head to a Christian college, SBC beliefs are at the core of a bunch of seminaries. Check out the schools at http://www.sbc.net/colleges.asp.

How can I hook up with this kind of Christianity?

The main way to find out about SBC Christianity is to visit their main website, and then use the "church search" link on the front page to locate a church near you: http://www.sbc.net/default.asp.

TRADITIONAL

GREEK ORTHODOX
Archdiocese of North America

THE SHORT LIST

WHAT'S THE 1-2-3 RANK FOR THINGS TO FOCUS ON?

- The traditions of Orthodox Christianity
- The personal experience you get from the sacraments (rituals)
- Scripture

WHAT'S THE BIBLE?

- A book inspired by God that's most accurate when read in its original languages

WHAT'S THE CHURCH LIKE?

- Influenced from the top down. Local churches run things along the lines of what main spiritual leaders say.

WHOM DO I CONTACT?

- 8 E. 79th St., New York, NY 10021
- Phone: (212) 570-3500; Fax (212) 570-3569
- URL: http://www.goarch.org/

When did this kind of Christianity get started?

Greek Orthodox churches teach a kind of Christianity where a person's relationship with God is based on ways that go back to the earliest years of the Christian Church. Greek Orthodox Christians say their kind of faith was formed even before the Bible was put together or different kinds of

Christian groups began to split off from one another. It's a traditional, conservative type of Christianity stressing rituals (sacraments) as the main ways Christians connect with God and preserve the faith.

The Greek Orthodox Church is known as an Eastern kind of Christianity. Back in the first days of the Christian Church, areas around the Mediterranean and the Middle East were about as Eastern as things got. Places like Asia just weren't on the radar yet in terms of Christianity, so the first Christian churches in places like Turkey, Egypt, Syria, or Greece were considered "Eastern."

Anyway, Eastern Christians—like Greek Orthodox believers—held a lot of pull when it came to nailing down what Christians have come to believe. Most of the early meetings church leaders had about things like what books went into the Bible were held in the East, and most church leaders at these meetings were Eastern Christians. They'd get together, decide on Christian beliefs, rituals, biblical interpretations, and a bunch of other stuff—then this info would make its way out to other churches.

But the early church eventually split into different groups. Western believers went one way and Eastern believers went another. (Check out the profile in this section for the Roman Catholic Church to read more about Western believers.) Today's Greek Orthodox Church is a part of the Eastern group. Basically it has kept things just like they were back in the early days, and even in the middle of twenty-first-century America sticks to the beliefs, rituals, and biblical interpretations decided on all those years ago.

Have I heard of them before?

It depends. Greek Orthodoxy is a church thing but it's also an ethnic thing. Orthodox churches have a lot to do with nationality, so they're better known among people of the particular nationality they represent than they are among people who aren't part of certain ethnic communities.

Greek Orthodoxy is well known among people of Greek or Mediterranean descent, but not always as well known to others. (Be sure to check out the links at the end of this chapter for Orthodox Christianity related to a different nationality: Russian Orthodoxy.)

What makes this kind of Christianity unique?

- Sacraments (rituals) are used to connect with God, the most important one being the main Orthodox service, the Divine Liturgy.
- Everything in Orthodox worship is done according to tradition.
- Greek Orthodox Christians work toward a kind of perfection known as theosis (thee-o-sis).
- It's common to hear teachings based on the writings of Christian saints (people given the gift of holiness by God) or priests alongside teachings from the Bible.

Is there a statement of faith (SOF)?

Greek Orthodoxy keeps it old-school, using historical confessions of faith. The Nicene Creed is the main creed, and people say the Lord's Prayer in almost all services.

Following are some of the main ideas and Bible verses a Greek Orthodox Church might focus on:

- Fasting prepares us properly for Christ's return: Matthew 9:14–15.
- Knowing Christ is a two-way relationship: Galatians 4:9.
- Prayer is a way of being, not just a way to talk with or request things from God: 1 Thessalonians 5:17, Matthew 6:7–8.
- We should imitate God and can become holy (or sainted) by participating in God's holiness: Leviticus 19:1–2, 2 Thessalonians 2:13–14.

Who's in charge?

The Ecumenical Patriarch of Constantinople (the EP) is the main spiritual leader Orthodox Christians look to for guidance, but he's not an official boss or anything.

Local Greek Orthodox churches run independently of the EP. People called primates, archbishops, and bishops are at the top of the ladder and do a lot of the church government stuff. Priests come next in terms of who's in charge and do things like performing services and rituals.

What's the word for people my age?

First, you've got GOYA: Greek Orthodox Youth of America. Different churches hold GOYA meetings so you can get with a local church on that.

Second, you've got a group called OCF, Orthodox Christian Fellowship. They run fellowship groups for Orthodox Christians on college campuses that you can check out here: http://www.ocf.net/index.asp.

Third, you can see what's up with the World Fellowship of Orthodox Youth, known as SYNDESMOS. The group is basically trying to bond together smaller youth movements and theological schools around the globe so they can collaborate. That's online at: http://www.syndesmos.org/en/.

Is there anything going on besides church?

If you're thinking it might be great to head to a Christian college, Greek Orthodox beliefs are at the core of colleges like this school: http://www.hchc.edu/.

You'll also find Greek Orthodox churches have a lot of cultural things happening that'll teach you more about what the kind of Christianity people practice at a Greek Orthodox church has to do with Greek culture, in general.

How can I hook up with this kind of Christianity?

The main way to find out about Greek Orthodox Christianity is to visit the Greek Orthodox Archdiocese of America website, since you can do everything there from finding a church in your area to reading up on the history of Greek Orthodoxy to chatting it up with others on a forum board. It's all at: http://www.goarch.org/.

Also, since Orthodox Christianity has a lot of nationality-based churches, take a look into Russian Orthodoxy too by checking out the Orthodox Church in America: http://www.oca.org/.

ROMAN CATHOLIC

THE SHORT LIST

WHAT'S THE 1-2-3 RANK FOR THINGS TO FOCUS ON?

- The traditions of Catholicism
- The personal experience you get from the sacraments (rituals)
- Scripture

WHAT'S THE BIBLE?

- An inspired record of revelation containing truths the Holy Ghost desired be written down

WHAT'S THE CHURCH LIKE?

- Controlled from the top down. Local churches run things according to what the Pope—or, main Catholic leader—says.

WHOM DO I CONTACT?

- 3211 Fourth St., Washington, DC 20017
- Phone: (202) 541-3000
- URL: http://www.vatican.va/

When did this kind of Christianity get started?

The Roman Catholic Church is known as a Western kind of Christianity. Since places like Asia just weren't on the radar yet in terms of Christianity, Christian churches located in places like Turkey, Egypt, Syria, or Greece were known as Eastern churches. Places like Italy, where the Roman

Catholic Church got its start, were considered Western.

Roman Catholics trace their history back to the moment when Christ founded His church on earth by saying to the apostle Peter, "On this rock I will build my church, and the power of death will not be able to defeat it" (Matthew 16:18; NCV). And Peter is considered the first leader of the Catholic Church.

Anyway, during the first years of Christianity you generally had church leaders meeting up to finalize things like Christian beliefs, what books went into the Bible, ways to interpret God's Word, and a bunch of other stuff. Then this info would make its way out to other churches. The bigger group of church leaders eventually split, and the Western Christians—like Roman Catholic believers—went their own direction, keeping things centered on Italy and on organizing their church around a single church leader like Peter was at the very start of the Roman Catholic Church. Today, that leader is known as the Pope.

Roman Catholicism didn't have any trouble staying true to that plan. It established itself on the world scene quickly. Most of the early explorers who discovered and began moving people to other continents outside Europe were working for the Catholic Church. And that's how Roman Catholicism got to America. After the first few explorers and missionaries, Roman Catholics became stable enough to even found their own state. Catholics who had come over from England founded Maryland in the seventeenth century (1600s) and began to spread across America from there.

Today's Roman Catholic Church has huge global influence. With sixty-five million Roman Catholics in America alone, Catholics are far and away the largest Christian group in the States. It's still expanding but stays true to its roots by keeping things organized the same way Christ and Peter are said to have set up the church all those years back.

Have I heard of them before?

Almost for sure. Roman Catholicism is major in terms of worldwide membership. In America it's the largest group of Christians and has the longest history in the country as being a single church without any split-offs.

What makes this kind of Christianity unique?

- One man leads the entire church worldwide—the Pope.
- Roman Catholics call Jesus' mom the Virgin Mary. She's considered a saint and shows up in a lot in church teachings.
- Everything in Roman Catholic worship is symbolic, and everything is done according to tradition.
- Sacraments (rituals) are used to connect with God at the weekly service Roman Catholics attend called Mass.

Is there a statement of faith (SOF)?

Roman Catholicism keeps it old-school, using historical confessions of faith. The Nicene and Apostles' Creeds are the main statements of belief and are matched up with the beliefs church leaders decide on when they meet up every so often for a Vatican Council.

Following are some of the main ideas and Bible verses a Roman Catholic church might focus on:

- The Church is where Jesus fulfills God's plan to unite all things in Him: Ephesians 1:10.
- The regular confession of sin is biblical and keeps our spiritual lives on track: Matthew 6:12, 1 John 1:9.
- Jesus isn't just symbolized in the Holy Eucharist (Communion), He's literally and wholly present: John 6:32–37, 1 Corinthians 10:16–17.

Who's in charge?

In a word: the Pope. Okay, that was two words, but you get what I'm saying.

Below the Pope, there are lots of councils, committees, and administrative offices that run, organize, and guide the majority of things worldwide for all Roman Catholic communities.

At the local level, deacons are at the start of the chain. They do things like preach or serve Holy Communion so long as they've had the proper training. Above deacons are priests. They've all been trained by the church to do the day-to-day stuff like weekly services, baptism, or other rituals. And then last, you've got bishops, the guys who oversee the bunches of churches located in the same area that get grouped together into something Roman Catholics call a diocese.

What's the word for people my age?

Life Teen is probably the best thing going for Roman Catholic youth. At their website you can visit forums, ask church leaders questions, find upcoming camps, training sessions, ministry and outreach opportunities, and various conferences. Also, Life Teen pairs up with local Roman Catholic communities, scheduling stops for the speaking tours and concerts Life Teen sponsors. Check it all out: http://www.lifeteen.org/index.asp.

Is there anything going on besides church?

Because Roman Catholicism is a worldwide movement, there's a mad amount of stuff going on—charity, education, hospitals, orphanages, homes for the elderly, etc. There's a little bit of everything, so it just depends on where a church is located and what kinds of needs are in that particular community.

Roman Catholics keep everyone in sync by doing the publishing thing. Visit the Web to read more at these Catholic news sites:

- *National Catholic Reporter:* http://www.natcath.com/
- *National Catholic Register:* http://www.ncregister.com/current/
- *Catholic World News:* http://www.cwnews.com/

If you're thinking it'd be great to head to a Christian college, Catholic beliefs are at the core of a bunch of colleges. Check out these schools: http://www.catholiccollegesonline.org/.

How can I hook up with this kind of Christianity?

The main way to find out about Roman Catholic Christianity is to visit the website of the Holy See in Vatican City, Italy, since the See is where all the Roman Catholic leadership comes from: http://www.vatican.va/phome_en.htm.

But if you want something a little smaller that's more a summary kind of deal, try this link: http://religiousmovements.lib.virginia.edu/nrms/ roman_catholicism.html.

If you like what you see, there's a parish locator to find a church near you: http://www.parishesonline.com/scripts/default.asp.

RUSSIAN ORTHODOX
The Orthodox Church in America

THE SHORT LIST

WHAT'S THE 1-2-3 RANK FOR THINGS TO FOCUS ON?

- The traditions of Russian Orthodox Christianity
- The personal experience you get from the sacraments (rituals)
- Scripture

WHAT'S THE BIBLE?

- The main written source of divine doctrine and the central guide to church worship

WHAT'S THE CHURCH LIKE?

- Influenced from the top down. Local churches run things along the lines of what main spiritual leaders have to say.

WHOM DO I CONTACT?

- P.O. Box 675, Syosset, NY 11791-0675
- Phone: (516) 922-0550; Fax (516) 922-0954
- URL: http://www.oca.org/

When did this kind of Christianity get started?

Christian Orthodox history ties itself back to the first churches and the earliest Christian fathers. As the Orthodox Church spread to various parts of the globe, nationally-based churches began to arise. These national churches stayed true to Orthodox doctrine, discipline, and spiritual practices but incorporated various hallmarks related to the people each church served. The Russian Orthodox Church came up out of this history.

The arrival of Russian Orthodoxy is a little newer, though. If we head back to 1867—before Alaska was even known as Alaska because it was still part of Russia—we run into Russian Orthodox monks working to establish their faith in various cities. In Kodiak, eight monks working on behalf of the Church of Russia set up headquarters and built the first Eastern Orthodox Church in North America. Over in the city of Sitka a cathedral goes up around this same time. And besides building projects, Russian Christians are creating an alphabet for the Aleutian (uh-loo-shun) language so Bibles can be translated in the language of the local people.

Fast-forward about a hundred years: Now Alaska is owned by the U.S., not Russia, and Russian Orthodox Christians have moved a little bit south. The center of the Russian Orthodox Church (the See) is now set up near San Francisco, California. The See is eventually moved again, though. To be closer to the immigrants the Russian Christians are serving, the See is packed up and moved from San Fran over to the East Coast. From New York City, the See is able to set up enough churches and communities to reach out to lots of Russian immigrants but also to other immigrants from countries like Serbia, Syria, and Bulgaria.

This outreach helps the church attract bigger numbers of members, give people the aid they need, develop stability, and get situated in a good way on the American scene.

Then, like a lot of religious groups gone big, people want to go different directions. This was due to huge political events shaking up Russia in the early 1900s. A revolutionary group took over the Russian state—when the state government went down the Russian Church suffered. Churches were intentionally destroyed, forcing believers to scatter, a lot of them to America.

Russian Christians in America begin to rethink the connections they've got to church leaders in Moscow. Some go their own way and form another group of Russian Orthodox Christians—the Russian Orthodox Church Outside Russia. Others hang tight. They organize their own affairs until things in Russia stabilize, and the revolution dies down, and they can get back in touch with church leaders in Moscow. The only hitch is that Orthodox Christians in America want the Russian church to give an okay to let American believers do their own thing. This idea doesn't really fly at first with church leaders back in Russia. Initially they resist. But eventually it's all good and the Russian Christians claiming a link to those first American Orthodox churches set up in Alaska get the right to govern their own affairs.

Today these independent churches are known as the Orthodox Church in America (OCA). Russian heritage and nationality are still a main part of the church, and so are the doctrines and spiritual practices of Christian Orthodoxy. History rules at OCA communities, and ties to the worldwide community of Orthodox Christians keep churches strong throughout time. Changes have been made here and there, but in general, the Orthodox Church in America draws strength from its historical foundation in ancient Christianity and in Russian culture.

Have I heard of them before?

Russian Orthodoxy is more a regional thing than anything else. Because OCA churches serve Russian and Russian-American believers, if you're not living in a neighborhood with that kind of influence you may have no idea the OCA church even exists. That said, if.you do live near an OCA church, there's some chance you've at least seen it. Many OCA churches are housed in huge, historical landmark buildings in old parts of major cities.

What makes this kind of Christianity unique?

- Leaders in Russian Orthodoxy are not infallible and don't have any rights or powers that others in the church can't challenge.
- The main way you connect with God in Russian Orthodoxy is through the weekly service, known as the Divine Liturgy.
- The writings of ancient Christian leaders, especially Saint John Chrysostom, are considered useful for Christian spirituality and are referred to a lot.
- Russian Orthodoxy teaches that we become ourselves only in God.

Is there a statement of faith (SOF)?

OCA churches don't do specific statements of faith since they rely more on historical confessions of Christianity. In particular, the Nicene Creed is a central part of Russian Orthodox belief.

Following are some of the main ideas and Bible verses a Russian Orthodox community might focus on:

- People are called to become what God is by nature. It's a process called theosis: Psalm 82:6, John 10:37.
- The seal of the gift of the Holy Spirit happens after baptism. It's called chrismation and is a mystery and a blessing.
- Russian Orthodox Christians do not follow the Pope, or connect their churches to Roman Catholicism.
- The Gospel is a treasure, brought to light by the Cross: Galatians 2:21.

Who's in charge?

OCA churches look to a guy called the Primate for spiritual direction. He keeps things on track in terms of Russian Orthodox values and beliefs, and other churches follow his lead on moral, social, and religious issues. Also, the Primate is in charge of staying in the loop with the worldwide Orthodox Christian scene.

Below the Primate, leaders like bishops are in charge of regional groups of OCA churches known as dioceses. And then each individual OCA church—known as a parish—has a rector and a priest. Priests perform liturgies and other worship-related services, while rectors are the general guides for the direction of the parish.

What's the word for people my age?

Though they're all connected in a way, each OCA church is really its own deal. What you'll find just depends on who runs things for people your age.

On a national level, though, the Youth, Young Adult, and Campus Ministry program (YYA) has you covered. If you head online to the YYA website, there's info on upcoming events and a general hub for figuring out what's up with Orthodox youth. It's all on the website: http://yya.oca.org/.

Is there anything going on besides church?

Because Russian Orthodox communities have strong cultural ties, you can always hook up with people promoting or preserving parts of Russian history and culture. This may be through food, dance, the arts, or another type of activity, but any of these cultural outlets will show you more about the specific link between Russian heritage and the Orthodox Church.

Orthodoxy is also well known for the place monks and nuns hold. It's a guy/girl thing that either gender can pursue, and most monastic communities are based on specific programs of spiritual development for the individual as well as social service or outreach. The Russian Orthodox community offers several monastic communities you can look into if you feel God's call. Start with:

http://www.oca.org/pages/ocaadmin/listings/monastics.html.

If you're thinking it might be great to head to a Christian college, Russian Orthodox beliefs are at the core of a few seminaries. Following is where to start checking things out:

- St. Tikhon's: http://www.stots.edu/
- St. Vladimir's: http://www.svots.edu/
- St. Herman's: http://www.alaskanchurch.org/shs/html/home.html

How can I hook up with this kind of Christianity?

The main way to find out about Russian Orthodoxy before you head off to visit a local church community is to visit the Orthodox Church in America (OCA) website. It's got church info for local communities, but also tons of stuff about Orthodox beliefs, history, and traditions: http://www.oca.org.

THE ARMENIAN CHURCH
Eastern

THE SHORT LIST

WHAT'S THE 1-2-3 RANK FOR THINGS TO FOCUS ON?

- The traditions of Armenian Christianity
- The personal experience you get from the sacraments (rituals)
- Scripture

WHAT'S THE BIBLE?

- The Word of God written by prophets and apostles, inspired by the Holy Spirit

WHAT'S THE CHURCH LIKE?

- Influenced from the top down. Local churches run things along the lines of what main spiritual leaders have to say.

WHOM DO I CONTACT?

- 630 Second Ave., New York, NY 10016
- Phone: (212) 686-0710
- URL: http://www.armenianchurch.org/

When did this kind of Christianity get started?

Before we get into when Armenian Christianity started, let's get into where Armenia is. On a map, I mean. It's easy to overlook. It's not a big country, and it's tucked among neighbors that are a lot more famous. Turkey and Iran are the famous neighbors on the Middle Eastern side of Armenia. Then Russia basically forms the border for the other side of Armenia. So it's a country with a few different cultural influences.

The religious history of the Armenian Church goes back to what's sometimes called the original church, or Christ's church as He preached in Jerusalem. And there are other Orthodox churches with this same history. Besides the Armenian Church, Greek, Syrian, Egyptian, and other Orthodox Christians tell the story of their national churches beginning with Christ. Each ties their church to the first days of the Christian faith.

For Armenian Christians, coming up with links to this kind of history is no problem. The apostles Thaddeus and Bartholomew are said to have taken Armenia by storm, preaching it up so often that the entire nation converted. In the year 301 Christianity became the state religion of Armenia. And by the year 314 Saint Gregory was running the first national church. Before people knew it, there was an Armenian alphabet being used to translate Scripture and an official Armenian version of the Bible.

The solid set-up laid down in the fourth century gave Armenian Orthodoxy a chance to grow. Saint Gregory's job running the national church turned into a supreme head of the church position from which other Armenian Christians could get spiritual direction, guidance, and structure. This centralized things and tailored Armenian Christianity to fit the Armenian culture. But there was a downside. Believers began to disagree about who the central leader should be and where they should look for leadership.

See, many Armenian Christians arrived in America to escape the political heat generating in countries around them. Once they arrived, believers had to think about the leaders and people they wanted to be tied to back home. Some Armenian Christians wanted to stick to what they'd always done and follow the leadership coming out of a place in Armenia called Etchmiadzin. Others weren't down. They started to look toward the leadership coming out of a place in Lebanon called Antelias.

In terms of religious belief and the way Armenian Christians worship, though, the split didn't make big waves. Armenian Orthodoxy has stayed consistent. In fact, its consistency is part of what makes this kind of Christianity a unique, recognizable kind of faith that continues to attract new members, while still serving and staying true to the Armenian culture the church is based on.

Have I heard of them before?

If you hang in Orthodox circles, like Greek or Russian Orthodox churches, there's a good chance you've heard something about the Armenian Church. Also, depending on where you live in the country, you might be close to one of the bigger centers of Armenian life and culture. Inland California, Massachusetts, Rhode Island, and some parts of New York City are examples of places like this. But in general, since Armenian Christianity has a lot to do with ethnic and cultural ties, it might be something new to you.

What makes this kind of Christianity unique?

- Worship isn't all about church leaders being at the altar or up on a stage. They move and mix among people as part of worship too.
- *Badarak* is the Armenian word for the Divine Liturgy, which is the main service in Orthodox Christian churches. Listen to sung portions of the Badarak online . . .

  ⏻ Hayr mer: http://www.arapian.com/audio/hairmer.mp3
  ⏻ Der voghormia:
  http://www.arapian.com/audio/dervoghormia.mp3
  ⏻ Urach ler: http://www.arapian.com/audio/ourachler.mp3

- Gospel readings tie together with Holy Communion, since both are ways Christ reveals Himself to believers.
- Fasting is an important preparation for worship.

Is there a statement of faith (SOF)?

The faith is linked to historical Christianity, so confessions used by early church fathers stay at the core of Armenian faith. The Nicene Creed is used, along with others.

Following are some of the main ideas and Bible verses an Armenian Orthodox community might focus on:

- Saint Gregory's life teaches Christians to live well. He's an example of proud Christian identity.
- Every song, prayer, and ritual is a reminder of Jesus as the Word: John 1:1.
- There is a supreme spiritual leader for Armenian Christians. But it's not the Pope. Roman Catholic Christianity is different from Orthodox Christianity.
- Being baptized is a privilege, not a right: Romans 6:3–4.

Who's in charge?

Depending on the group of Armenian Christians you're in, the ultimate leader is a spiritual guide living in Armenia. He's called the Catholicos of All Armenians and is elected by church leaders. If you snag the Catholicos job, it's a lifetime deal, and the main responsibility of the job is to guide Armenian Orthodoxy toward God's plan for the church and toward faithfulness.

Local Armenian churches follow the lead of the Catholicos. They also listen up for decisions made by the Council of Bishops, since that council defines worship styles, beliefs, rules, and other things Armenian churches are all supposed to follow. Then bishops, priests, and deacons put all this stuff in motion, working together to run things from day to day at local churches (called parishes).

What's the word for people my age?

Armenian churches feature tons of singing. So choir groups are pretty easy to find and hook up with on the local level. Just ask around.

As for national stuff, Armenian Christianity is split between coasts. This means there's an Armenian Church Youth Organization group on both sides of the country. If you're on the West Coast, try this link: http://www.acyo-wd.org. If you're more central or East Coast, go here: http://www.acyoa.org.

Both sites list parish events, regional retreats, meetings, conferences, camps, and general news about the Armenian scene for people your age. There are also photos from the stuff going on and updates about things like college or service projects.

Is there anything going on besides church?

Armenian Orthodox churches merge Christian beliefs with Armenian culture and heritage. That means you'll always find cultural outlets that will show you more about the specific way Armenian culture has influenced Orthodox Christianity.

One of these outlets is CYMA—the Christian Youth Mission to Armenia. It's a way to get believers back in touch with Armenia as a country while also learning about mission work, preaching, evangelism, and Christian tradition. All the info is online at: http://www.cyma-wd.org/main.htm.

Family heritage and history is another outlet for the preservation of culture in the Armenian Church. A website full of links can get you started to see what ties you might have to history: http://www.armenianchurch.org/heritage/history/geneology.html.

If you're thinking it might be great to head to a Christian college, Armenian beliefs are something people are talking about online. Discussion groups help sort out college issues and give ideas for school, faith, and life. Check out this site: http://www.armenianchurch.org/301/connect/index.html.

How can I hook up with this kind of Christianity?

The main way to find out about Armenian Orthodoxy before you head off to visit a local church community is to visit the Web. West Coast things are up at: http://www.armenianchurchwd.com/maineng.htm. East Coast (and central) things are over at: http://www.armenianchurch.org.

Either site can get you info on your local area, but give a look at the history and other pages at each website to get a full picture of the Armenian Church.

ECSTATIC

ASSEMBLIES OF GOD

THE SHORT LIST

WHAT'S THE 1-2-3 RANK FOR THINGS TO FOCUS ON?

- Personal experience you get from the baptism of the Holy Spirit
- Scripture
- The traditions of Assemblies of God Christianity

WHAT'S THE BIBLE?

- A book inspired by God that's the infallible, final word when it comes to what's what in faith and life

WHAT'S THE CHURCH LIKE?

- Teamed up with others. Churches choose to cooperate with each other and keep the same values and beliefs.

WHOM DO I CONTACT?

- General Council of the Assemblies of God
- 1445 North Boonville Ave., Springfield, MO 65802-1894
- Phone: (417) 862-2781
- URL: http://ag.org/top/

When did this kind of Christianity get started?

Assemblies of God (A/G) churches are part of the Pentecostal Movement. Pentecostal Christians believe the Holy Spirit gives Christians a kind of personal, spiritual power that's visible to others. They believe the Spirit shows Himself when people do things like heal others, talk in tongues (a spiritual language), or get the ability to perform miracles.

You can probably guess that Pentecostals get their name from the Pentecost story in the book of Acts. And though lots of other kinds of Christians believe in this story and in the Holy Spirit being poured out on believers, Pentecostal Christians are more focused on the Spirit's role in the story than other Christians. Before Pentecostalism got rolling, nobody was really running around trying to say they had the kinds of powers the Spirit gave people at Pentecost. Why not? Well, that's exactly what Pentecostals asked since it definitely seemed like people receiving powers of the Spirit was something right off the pages of the Bible and a gift from God. A lot of Christians started to ask: Why can't people still get that kind of stuff now?

So eventually the powers of Pentecost were something lots of Christians started to take seriously. People started studying and praying, and eventually concluded that Christians really could be baptized in the Spirit just like in the story. It wasn't a one-time miracle deal that didn't happen anymore, and when people were baptized in the Spirit, others could see what happened. The baptism gave Christians things like the ability to heal others, talk in tongues, or perform miracles. A famed preacher named William J. Seymour took these beliefs big-time in the early twentieth century (the 1900s) by holding a revival to convert people all across Los Angeles, California. Just like he believed—and just like the Pentecost story in Acts—people converted and were overcome with the Spirit, showing all kinds of spiritual gifts. The Pentecostal Movement took off from there and ever since then has been a kind of Christianity where people focus on spiritual gifts and on growing in faith by expressing them.

All this Pentecostal stuff is the backstory to the kind of Christianity A/G believers practice and kind of what was going on West-Coast style at the turn of the century. But A/G as its own deal is a Midwestern thing. In southern states like Arkansas, Spirit-filled preachers and their followers were setting up local church communities, but they didn't all work together. So with all the church start-ups going on, it was then or never to get everybody together into some kind of cooperative fellowship. About three hundred preachers and church members from America and abroad did that by incorporating themselves as the General Council of the Assemblies of God. The council helped the A/G church rise out of the Midwest, since it clearly defined the beliefs particular to A/G Christians having to do with things like sanctification (becoming holy) and conversion. With clearly defined beliefs and a statement of faith everybody could agree to, lots of different A/G communities could now be on the same page, helping the movement expand. Today A/G is still growing and has gone global, becoming the "it" group when it comes to overall size and membership numbers among Pentecostal Christian groups.

Have I heard of them before?

Almost for sure. A/G churches are seriously everywhere. Small towns have 'em. Big cities have 'em. There are A/G megachurches and A/G churches as small as a weekly home study group. Because of how many A/G Christians there are, it's likely that you've heard something about them or seen an A/G church in your area.

What makes this kind of Christianity unique?

- Singing is key at most A/G churches—everything from traditional hymns to worship music to regional songs or old-school gospel and spiritual music.
- Those who are sick are anointed with oil, or brought forward so others can lay hands on them for healing and spiritual power.
- Expressions of the Spirit are cool. Don't worry about hiding them, since they're blessings—tongues, prophesying, healing, or whatever.

Is there a statement of faith (SOF)?

A/G churches use the Statement of Fundamental Truths, which was written back in the day when the church was just getting started. You can read the whole thing online at: http://ag.org/top/beliefs/truths.cfm.

Following are some of the main ideas and Bible verses an A/G church might focus on:

- After being born again, Christians are entitled to and should definitely seek baptism in the Holy Ghost and fire: Acts 1:4, 8, 1 Corinthians 12:1–31, Luke 24:29.
- God is one single "I AM," but can represent three different principles in order to relate to us: Father, Son, and Holy Ghost: Deuteronomy 6:4, Isaiah 43:10, 11, Matthew 28:19, Luke 3:22.
- Character counts. Biblical virtues like truth, integrity, and self-control are central to living a godly—not a worldly—life.

Who's in charge?

The A/G system kinda puts two people in charge on a local level. There's a pastor, who runs the day-to-day things at each church; and a district officer, who's responsible for the promotion of home missions for all the churches that are bunched together to form one particular A/G district.

At the top of the A/G, church officers meet every two years with a group of A/G pastors and church members for something called the General Council, where doctrine is decided and passed along to all the partner churches.

What's the word for people my age?

Since each A/G community is its own deal, what you'll find just depends on who runs things for people your age.

On a national level, the A/G Church runs the National Youth Ministries (NYM), which is a place you can look to find out about missions, arts and creative outlets, festivals, conferences, and camps: http://youth.ag.org/.

Is there anything going on besides church?

Missionaries are a main form of outreach, since evangelism is such a big deal in A/G Christianity. There are U.S. missions and global missions as well as mission efforts that use literature or media or other specific evangelization tools to get God's Word out. An overview of the whole A/G missions package is at:
http://ag.org/top/section_missions.cfm.

If you're thinking it'd be great to head to a Christian college, A/G Christianity is at the core of a bunch of schools:
http://colleges.ag.org/college_guide/index.cfm.

How can I hook up with this kind of Christianity?

The main way to find out about A/G Christianity is to visit their main website: http://ag.org/top/.

CHARISMATIC CATHOLICS

THE SHORT LIST

WHAT'S THE 1-2-3 RANK FOR THINGS TO FOCUS ON?

- The personal experience you get from the Holy Spirit
- The traditions of Catholic Christianity
- Scripture

WHAT'S THE BIBLE?

- Sacred books written and collected over time that guide and direct us

WHAT'S THE CHURCH LIKE?

- Influenced from the top down. Local churches run things along the lines of what main spiritual leaders have to say.

WHOM DO I CONTACT?

- No central organization or office. Look up your local Catholic diocese in the phone book and ask how to locate a charismatic group near you.

When did this kind of Christianity get started?

Charismatic Catholicism isn't a movement that just up and started one day. That's because it's a modern blend of two things: the gifts and graces of the Holy Spirit and the traditions of the Catholic Church. The fusion took time. It started with individuals, expanded to small groups, and is now a growing movement many Catholics are reading up on or joining.

When you tie Christianity directly together with the gifts of the Holy Spirit, it's a style of belief made popular by Pentecostal Christians. And that's kind of where the Charismatic Catholic Movement gets confusing. So you have Catholics, right? Then you've got Protestants (the Pentecostals), right? The two kinds of Christianity usually have a big gap between them. Protestants are believers who went Martin Luther's way back in the Middle Ages and ditched out on doing things Catholic style. Catholics are a historical, traditional group of believers who stayed the course when Luther and other Protestants began worshiping in a different way. So when we get to the start of Charismatic Catholicism as a movement, we're actually going back in time. Instead of Catholics and Protestants living apart, with a gap between them, Charismatic Catholicism blends the two. Believers speak in tongues, practice prophesying, and encourage worship to be an emotional experience. But they also keep up with Catholic traditions too. Charismatic Catholics take Communion, participate in other sacraments (rituals), and still organize the church according to what's sent down by Roman Catholic leaders like the Pope.

Though people had been having individual charismatic experiences in the 1960s, particularly among college students at schools like Duquesne and Notre Dame, a Catholic leader named Cardinal Suenens is said to have experienced the gifts of the Holy Spirit in such a powerful way that he was led to promote this kind of Catholic spirituality for the rest of his life. This was back in the 1970s. Cardinal Suenens was so moved that he talked up the experience and inspired other Catholics to open themselves up to new ideas. With time, prayer, and more individual experiences like Suenens's, the idea of putting more emphasis on spiritual gifts took hold. It became a movement based on renewal, the Holy Spirit making believers new. So Charismatic Catholics began to call their kind of belief and worship the Charismatic Catholic Renewal Movement.

In America, Charismatic Catholicism has proved popular. It's not a huge movement, but it's been stable. The movement was hot during the 1970s, and though it has cooled down a bit, Catholic believers continue to be into it. The movement has grown little bits at a time. The global picture of Charismatic Catholicism is a bit bigger. It's pretty common to find Holy Spirit-centered worshipers among Catholic believers in countries from Malaysia to Australia. So as time goes on, the Charismatic Renewal Movement is likely to stay put on the Christian scene.

Have I heard of them before?

There's no single, central hub for Charismatic Catholics, and it's not a giant movement sweeping the country. So having heard about them is hit or miss. Local Catholic churches might advertise that they do things in a Charismatic style, but there's no guarantee. In general, you'll probably hear about Charismatic Catholic communities only if you keep an ear to the ground in Pentecostal or Catholic circles.

What makes this kind of Christianity unique?

- Roman Catholic tradition, ritual, and organization are followed, but worship is modern and high energy.
- Collaborating with other Christians in unity is a main goal for Charismatic Catholic groups.
- The Pope is the spiritual leader of the Charismatic Catholics, even though the Holy Spirit focus of the group is based on Protestant ideas.
- Healing, prophesying, and speaking in tongues are common things to see at Charismatic Catholic services.

Is there a statement of faith (SOF)?

Because Charismatic Catholics remain part of the Roman Catholic Church, each community stands by the historical creeds of the Catholic Church but has additional statements on the specific work of the Holy Spirit.

Following are some of the main ideas and Bible verses a Charismatic Catholic community might focus on:

- Spiritual gifts (called charisms) are something we should desire: 1 Corinthians 14.
- Charismatic spirituality is a return to the personal encounter with the Spirit of God, not something new: Acts 2.
- People using their individual charisms is what allows the body of Christ to reach its full potential: Ephesians 4:15–16.
- Saint Peter and Saint Paul represent Christian lives moved and guided by the role of the Holy Spirit. They can be thought of as patron saints of the Charismatic Renewal Movement.

Who's in charge?

Charismatic Catholics are no different from other kinds of Catholic believers in terms of spiritual leadership. All look to Vatican City in Italy and to the worldwide leader of the Roman Catholic Church the Pope.

At the local level, Catholic priests who are trained and educated for the position run the day-to-day services and events. So if a local priest is interested in using Charismatic worship styles or promoting Charismatic beliefs, he may do so with the approval of the leaders in his area (or diocese).

What's the word for people my age?

Though Roman Catholic churches support organizations like Life Teen (http://www.lifeteen.org/) and other young-adult programs, Charismatic-based activities just depend on who runs things at your local church (or parish).

Is there anything going on besides church?

Charismatic Catholic communities aren't any different from regular Roman Catholic churches when it comes to things going on. Social service work is a key part of the Catholic faith, but besides reaching out through charity and aid, Charismatic Catholics also focus on promoting Christian unity. This might be in the form of local prayer meetings, home worship services, or neighborhood projects the church teams up with others to complete.

Also, Charismatic renewals in faith have led to a kind of lifestyle renewal you can participate in, even if it's just as a volunteer. Christians interested to see what effect they can have on one another and the wider world are choosing to live in small communities. There, life and faith are tied together as people work and serve side by side. Check out the Living Water Community for an example:
http://www.livingwatercommunity.com/.

If you're thinking it might be great to head to a Christian college, Catholic beliefs are at the core of a bunch of schools. You'll just have to sort out what kind of place Charismatic ideas and beliefs hold at the schools you're interested in:
http://www.catholiccollegesonline.org/.

How can I hook up with this kind of Christianity?

The main way to find out about Charismatic Catholicism before you head off to visit a local church community is to do a bit of research. Go to the source and check out the writings of Cardinal Suenens. His ideas, work, and pastoral care led to so much of what's going on today in the Charismatic Renewal Movement. You'll have a way more informed view of what's up before you visit a community if you get hold of Suenens's work.

When you're ready to see what Charismatic Catholics are like, use the websites below to find a group near you, or try calling your local Catholic diocese office. Ask for a referral to a Charismatic church and see what you come up with:

 The Catholic Fraternity International: http://www.catholicfraternity.net/index.html

 NewFrontiers: http://www.newfrontiers.xtn.org/index.php

CHURCH OF THE NAZARENE

THE SHORT LIST

WHAT'S THE 1-2-3 RANK FOR THINGS TO FOCUS ON?

- Scripture
- Personal experience you get from the baptism of the Holy Spirit
- The traditions of Methodist and Holiness Christianity

WHAT'S THE BIBLE?

- A guide that directs each person's conscience

WHAT'S THE CHURCH LIKE?

- Teamed up with others. Churches cooperate with one another and keep the same values and beliefs.

WHOM DO I CONTACT?

- 6401 The Paseo, Kansas City, MO 64131
- Phone: (816) 333-7000
- URL: http://www.nazarene.org/

When did this kind of Christianity get started?

Nazarene Christianity has a lot of people to thank in terms of having gotten off and running on its own. Here's how it breaks down: You've got a Protestant kind of Christianity called Methodism, dating to 1750. Then inside Methodist Christianity you've got a group of people who want to emphasize Christian teachings about holiness and perfection, more so than other Methodist believers do. Not surprisingly, these people pick up the name Holiness Christians. And it's from this group of Holiness Christians that Nazarene Christianity takes off and gets going.

To sum things up for these other Christian groups Nazarene Christianity develops out of, it's best to start with Minister John Wesley (d. 1791). He's at the center of Methodist Christianity and preached a set of particular ideas about prayer, fasting, Bible reading, and doing charitable works that were a kind of *method* for Christian living. At the center of his method was a personal experience of conversion with a lot of emphasis on the potential for holiness in a Christian's life. Wesley was talking about really personal, really individual stuff.

A lot of the people who followed these teachings took them to mean that a Christian could focus on personal sanctification and on becoming perfect, like Christ. Not all the Christians following Wesley's teachings focused so much on this part, though. Some kept following Wesley's method without the sanctification and perfection parts. But the others who wanted to focus on this stuff eventually broke away and did their own thing. They focused on being holy so much that the movement was called Holiness Christianity.

So out of these Holiness Christians was where Nazarene Christianity sprang up. A bunch of Holiness churches, missions, and associations grouped together and formed their own official kind of Christianity. A preacher named Phineas F. Bresee was behind the push to get everyone together and organized the first group to use the name Church of the Nazarene. This was out on the West Coast but eventually attracted the attention of people doing the holiness thing on the East Coast and in the South too. Christians from all these areas eventually hooked up and today go by the name Nazarene Christians.

Have I heard of them before?

Maybe. The Church of the Nazarene balances social and spiritual issues, so there's a chance you've run into Nazarene Christians either helping out in an outreach kind of way, or you might have run into a Nazarene Christian evangelist.

The only part that decreases the chance you've heard about the group is because of how conservative Nazarene beliefs are. With an emphasis on holiness and perfection, a lot of Nazarene Christians aren't hanging out doing the pop-culture thing. Drinking, movies, and stuff like that are sometimes big no-no's, which means you're probably not going to run into a Nazarene Christian kicking it at the mall or partying or whatever.

What makes this kind of Christianity unique?

- Though there's a lot of emphasis on the Holy Spirit, Nazarene Christianity doesn't get into the spiritual gift of tongues like Pentecostal Christian groups do.
- Nazarene Christianity has been okay with women being ordained from the get-go.
- Nazarene Christians believe the Holy Spirit does a second work in us after conversion. It's this second deal that can ultimately ditch our sin and renew us in the image of God.

Is there a statement of faith (SOF)?

The Church of the Nazarene lives by its Articles of Faith. Also, church communities use something called the Eight Agreed Statements: http://www.nazarene.org/welcome/beliefs/index.html.

Following are some of the main ideas and Bible verses a Church of the Nazarene community might focus on:

- Through Christ, Christians can have a more loving, patient, self-disciplined life that's in line with God's perfect nature: 2 Corinthians 3:18, Galatians 5:22–23, 1 John 3:2.
- The Holy Spirit is the counselor Jesus promised and left in His place after leaving the earth: John 7:37–39.
- Baptism is a must-do, but you can be sprinkled, dunked, or whatever. It's up to you, and baptism can be done as a kid or an adult. There's no age requirement.

Who's in charge?

Though pastors do the day-to-day stuff, local Church of the Nazarene communities are kept organized and on track by district and general superintendents. And then at the tiptop of Nazarene Christianity you've got a General Assembly where representatives from different Nazarene church communities get together and decide on all the official stuff that's going to be nailed down for the year.

What's cool, though, is that everybody gets a say in what goes on at the General Assembly. The perspectives of church leaders and regular community members are all represented, making it an even-steven kind of deal.

What's the word for people my age?

Since each Church of the Nazarene community is its own deal, what you'll find just depends on who runs things for people your age.

The big thing to look into is the National Youth Institute (NYI). It connects Nazarene Christians worldwide, and the NYI website has tools you can use to post questions and talk with people on the forum board, and find out about retreats, missions trips, and conferences that are coming up. NYI's website is: http://nyi.nazarene.org/index.php?menu=For+Youth.

Is there anything going on besides church?

The Church of the Nazarene isn't kidding around when it comes to evangelization and world missions. Check out these different sites to see how global it all gets:

Nazarene World Mission: http://www.nazareneworldmission.org/mainsite.html

Nazarene Missions International: http://www.nazarenemissions.org/

USA and Canada Missions: http://www.usamission.org/

Nazarene Compassionate Ministries International: http://www.ncm.org/index.html

Jesus Film Trips: http://www.jfhp.org/getinvolved/trips.html

If you're thinking it might be great to head to a Christian college, Nazarene Christianity is at the core of a bunch of schools: http://www.usamission.org/colleges.html.

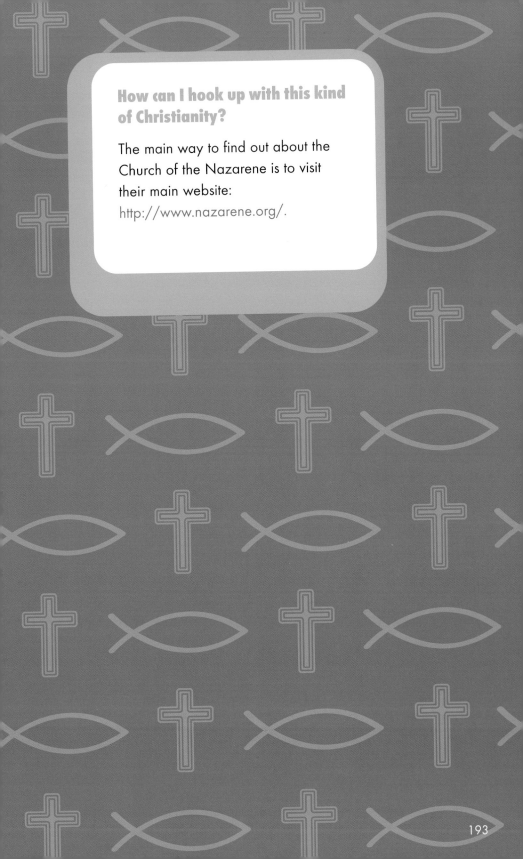

How can I hook up with this kind of Christianity?

The main way to find out about the Church of the Nazarene is to visit their main website: http://www.nazarene.org/.

INTERNATIONAL CHURCH OF THE FOURSQUARE GOSPEL

THE SHORT LIST

WHAT'S THE 1-2-3 RANK FOR THINGS TO FOCUS ON?

- Personal experience you get from the baptism of the Holy Spirit
- Scripture
- The traditions of Foursquare Christianity

WHAT'S THE BIBLE?

- A book that's true, absolute, and unchangeable

WHAT'S THE CHURCH LIKE?

- Teamed up with others. Churches cooperate with one another and keep the same values and beliefs.

WHOM DO I CONTACT?

- 1910 W. Sunset Blvd., Ste. 200, Los Angeles, CA 90026-0176
- Phone: (213) 989-4500; Fax (213) 989-4538
- URL: http://www.foursquare.org/

When did this kind of Christianity get started?

Foursquare churches grew from the small evangelical efforts of one woman, Aimee Semple McPherson, into a still-expanding kind of Christianity that's organized around the

Holy Spirit and simple living. Obviously, it was kind of out of the norm for a woman to be preaching back in the 1900s, but Semple McPherson did a lot of things out of the norm. Not only did she get Foursquare rolling on her own, but she also did things like start a radio station and pastor a church of more than five thousand people. She preached about heaven being a place Christians should shoot for, and about Christians' setting up their lives around serving Jesus. Semple McPherson also preached equality among people, evangelized minority groups who were segregated at that time in history, and basically delivered God's Word through optimistic positivity, focusing on the good rather than on shaming people or making them feel bad.

Pentecostal ideas also show up in Foursquare Christianity, as Semple McPherson preached that Christians living right should be proud of the spiritual gifts they've received from God. She lived during the same time as the famed preacher who put Pentecostal Christianity on the map in a big way, a guy named William J. Seymour. His preaching about the spiritual gifts Christians could receive and the Holy Spirit baptism that was available to all Christians, just like in the Pentecost story in Acts, made a big noise on the West Coast during the early 1900s. Semple McPherson was smack-dab in the same spot and passed along some of these ideas in her messages too.

Overall, the Foursquare message was supposed to be simple and easy to follow, which gave Foursquare Christianity a rep for being a kind of faith that combined God's Word with a specific plan for living that was arranged in a step-by-step format. The blessings of God were preached as the natural result of following the plan. And that's still what's preached today.

Have I heard of them before?

It depends. Foursquare churches have deep roots in large metropolitan, urban, and downtown areas of different cities. If you live in one of these types of places, you may know what's up with Foursquare.

Also, Foursquare's history and relationship to Pentecostal Christianity means you may know what's up if you hang in Pentecostal circles, because you might have been exposed to Foursquare through a church visit, a youth group function for Pentecostal teens, etc.

What makes this kind of Christianity unique?

- The Foursquare name is based on there being four things Christianity is all about:
    1. Christ as Savior (soul),
    2. Baptized with the Holy Spirit (spirit),
    3. Great Physician (body), and
    4. The soon-coming King (eternity).
- Evangelism is a huge part of Foursquare Christianity, especially the effort to translate God's Word into people's own languages.
- Foursquare churches are okay with women working at any level of church leadership.
- Foursquare Christianity is designed to be plain and easy to understand.

Is there a statement of faith (SOF)?

The Foursquare Declaration of Faith, written by Foursquare founder Aimee Semple McPherson, is still used today. You can read the whole thing online at: http://www.foursquare.org/index.cfm?cat=about&subcat=believe&subsubcat=doctrine.

Following are some of the main ideas and Bible verses a Foursquare church might focus on:

- The power of Christ to heal the physically sick is a kind of divine healing, and it's an answer to prayers of faith: James 5:14–16.
- The Lord's Supper (Communion) is a symbolic act, not anything that literally brings Jesus into the bread or juice of the vine: 1 Corinthians 11:24–25.
- Winning souls for Christ is the first and most important responsibility of the church: James 5:20.

Who's in charge?

At the local level, teachings, beliefs, and doctrine are pretty much the same from church to church and are directed by a pastor. Everybody gets a say in what goes on at Foursquare churches.

Then the big tiptop event in the church is the Annual Convention, where different Foursquare members and leaders get to vote on issues related to things for the partner churches.

What's the word for people my age?

Since each Foursquare community is its own deal, what you'll find just depends on who runs things for people your age.

In terms of Foursquare worldwide, the National Foursquare Youth Ministry (NFYM) runs a website that's got everything from event lists to tips for college to camps you can attend: http://www.foursquare.org/redirect.cfm?http://www.nfym.com.

Is there anything going on besides church?

Foursquare isn't kidding around when it comes to ministries and missions. They run a ton of things inside the church that support various groups or kinds of Foursquare Christians. Link to the complete list: http://www.foursquare.org/index.cfm?cat=us&subcat=departments.

After the in-church stuff, Foursquare goes big-time when it comes to missions. They have everything from youth-centered missions where you'll team up with a pastor/mentor to get God's work done, to traditional missionary and church planting efforts. Following is the whole deal: http://www.foursquare.org/index.cfm?cat=missions.

If you're thinking it might be great to head to a Christian college, Foursquare's Life Pacific College might be something you're into: http://www.lifepacific.edu/.

How can I hook up with this kind of Christianity?

The main way to find out about Foursquare Christianity is to visit their main website: http://foursquare.org.

If you want more of a summary about Foursquare Christianity in general, try: http://religiousmovements.lib.virginia.edu/nrms/Foursqu.html.

THE CHURCH OF GOD IN CHRIST

THE SHORT LIST

WHAT'S THE 1-2-3 RANK FOR THINGS TO FOCUS ON?

- Personal experience you get from the baptism of the Holy Spirit
- Scripture
- The traditions of Church of God in Christ Christianity

WHAT'S THE BIBLE?

- An infallible system of doctrine that's got all bases covered for Christians

WHAT'S THE CHURCH LIKE?

- Controlled from the top down. Local churches run things according to what main spiritual leaders say.

WHOM DO I CONTACT?

- 272 S. Main St., Memphis, TN 38101
- URL: http://cogic.org/

When did this kind of Christianity get started?

Pentecostal Christianity is the movement that gave the Church of God in Christ its foundation and its start. Pentecostal beliefs about the Spirit showing itself when people do things like heal others, talk in tongues (a spiritual language), or get the ability to perform miracles recalls the Pentecost story from the book of Acts. Before Pentecostalism got rolling, nobody was really running around trying to say they had the kinds of powers the Spirit gave people at Pentecost. But people started studying and praying, and eventually concluded that Christians really could be baptized in the Spirit, just like in the story. It wasn't a one-time miracle deal that didn't happen anymore, and when people were baptized in the Spirit, others could see what happened. One of the most famous people to pray, study, and promote these ideas was a preacher named William J. Seymour. His West Coast revivals were full of people who converted to Christ and then, overcome with the Spirit, showed all kinds of spiritual gifts.

The Pentecostal Movement took off from there and is the backstory to the kind of Christianity COGIC believers practice. Charles H. Mason, the founder of the COGIC, was at Seymour's So-Cal revivals and experienced the spiritual gift of tongues for himself. So convinced, moved, and inspired by what he'd been through, Mason became a preacher focused on getting the word out that other Christians could experience the same thing.

Mason preached about the ability of all Christians to receive spiritual gifts as part of their walk of faith. He headed home to Memphis, Tennessee, and began to preach his message as a New Testament doctrine to African-Americans like himself. Soon after that a group of pastors who understood what Mason had to say teamed up with him, all getting together to form the first Pentecostal General Assembly of the COGIC.

Today the COGIC is all about the Holy Spirit (usually called the Holy Ghost) and has become the main kind of Pentecostal Christianity for African-Americans, which sets it apart from other Pentecostal groups like the Assemblies of God.

Have I heard of them before?

It depends. COGIC Christianity is huge among African-American Christians, but isn't as well known among other racial groups like Asians, Hispanics, or Caucasians.

Also, COGIC's history and relationship to Pentecostal Christianity mean you may know what's up if you hang in Pentecostal circles.

What makes this kind of Christianity unique?

- Worship is intense, loud, and hyped at COGIC churches. Shouting stuff like "Yes, Lord!" or "Hallelujah!" during service is all good.
- Women have their own kind of leader. A National Supervisor of Women goes by the title "Mother" and provides spiritual leadership, direction, and guidance for all women in COGIC churches.
- COGIC churches teach that the Holy Ghost gradually ditches the sin inside a believer and renews his or her nature.

Is there a statement of faith (SOF)?

There's an official COGIC statement of faith that each local COGIC community uses. If you want to read through it, visit this website: http://www.cogic.org/believe.htm.

Following are some of the main ideas and Bible verses a COGIC church might focus on:

- After converting, if Christians receive the ability to speak in tongues, it's proof they've been baptized in the Holy Ghost: Acts 1:8, 8:39, John 16:13.
- Demons are real. They're unclean spirits that can be embodied in human beings, but Christians can conquer and overcome this kind of evil: Mark 16:17.
- Miracles occur to convince people that the Bible is God's Word, and miracles still occur today.

Who's in charge?

On a local level, each church runs itself with a pastor doing all the day-to-day stuff, but it looks to the overall spiritual leader of the COGIC for direction. This position began with COGIC founder Charles H. Mason and has been filled since his death by different COGIC bishops as the years have gone by.

Then you've also got the General Board, which is a twelve-man governing body that takes care of the international COGIC.

What's the word for people my age?

Since each COGIC community is its own deal, what you'll find just depends on who runs things for people your age. Give this website a look as an example: http://www.newwayexp.org/index.php.

On a global level, you can visit the website COGIC runs for their International Youth Department: http://www.cogicyouth.com/.

And while you're online, head over to check out this link with info about cool stuff going on in terms of keeping young COGIC members committed to purity: http://www.purityclass.com/.

Is there anything going on besides church?

The COGIC Department of Missions is huge. There's just no better way to say it. See what's going on at: http://www.cogicmissions.org/.

Related to missions efforts is the International Department of Evangelism. Saving souls is tied into missions work for COGIC Christians, both in the United States and abroad. Following what's up with that: http://www.cogicevangelism.com/.

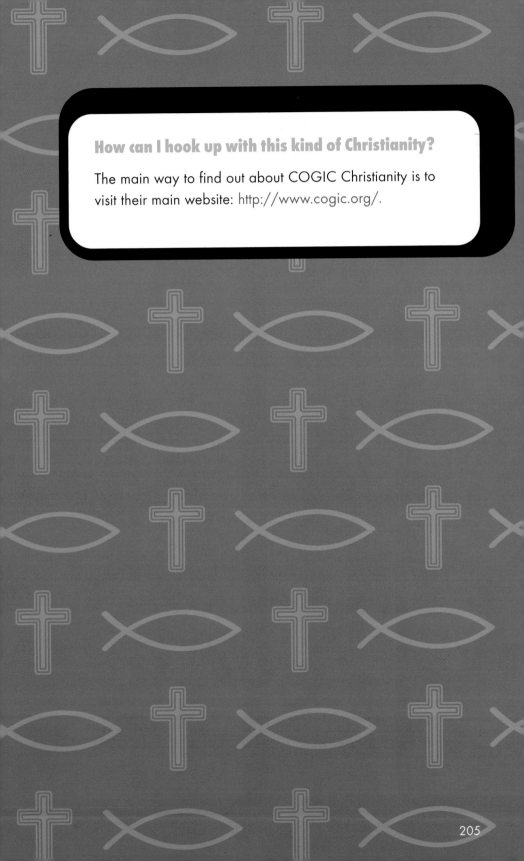

How can I hook up with this kind of Christianity?

The main way to find out about COGIC Christianity is to visit their main website: http://www.cogic.org/.

VINEYARDUSA
The Vineyard

THE SHORT LIST

WHAT'S THE 1-2-3 RANK FOR THINGS TO FOCUS ON?

- Personal experience Christians get from the baptism of the Holy Spirit
- Scripture
- The traditions of Pentecostal Christianity

WHAT'S THE BIBLE?

- The final authority for Christian faith and practice

WHAT'S THE CHURCH LIKE?

- Teamed up with others. Churches cooperate with each other and keep the same values and beliefs.

WHOM DO I CONTACT?

- P.O. Box 2089, Stafford, TX 77497
- Phone: (281) 313-8463
- URL: http://vineyardusa.org/

When did this kind of Christianity get started?

Vineyard churches are a recent Christian group basically taking shape in the 1970s. They draw on a lot of ideas associated with Pentecostal Christianity. Pentecostal Christians believe the Holy Spirit gives Christians a kind of personal, spiritual power that's visible to others and that the Spirit shows Himself when people do things like heal others, talk in tongues (a spiritual language), or get the ability to perform miracles.

The name Pentecostal comes from the story of Pentecost in the book of Acts. Before Pentecostalism got rolling, nobody was really running around trying to say they had the kinds of powers the Spirit gave people at Pentecost. But eventually some Christians started to take these ideas seriously, believing that a baptism in the Spirit gave Christians gifts like the ability to heal others, talk in tongues, or perform miracles. A famed preacher named William J. Seymour took these beliefs big-time in the early twentieth century (the 1900s), and though the Vineyard isn't directly tied to Seymour or the Pentecostal Movement that grew out of his teachings, the Vineyard encourages a lot of the same ideas.

The big catch is that the Vineyard developed gradually through the teachings of a pastor named Kenn Gulliksen. He was a pastor who was really into emphasizing the gifts of the Holy Spirit. Other pastors of the church he was preaching in weren't, so Gulliksen went his own way and promoted Spirit-filled worship and individual gifts on his own, gathering believers as he continued to preach. Another pastor, John Wimber, turned out to be doing the same thing in the same area, so the two of them hooked up, eventually leading to Vineyard-style Christianity.

Today, the Vineyard Movement is huge. There's a VineyardUSA, a Vineyard Canada, a Vineyard UK, and more. The movement has expanded quickly, and it continues to pick up members and be popular on the Christianity scene.

Have I heard of them before?

It depends. Because the first Vineyard churches were offshoots of Calvary Chapel churches, a lot of evangelical Christians moved from one side of the boat to the other. If you hang in evangelical circles, you might know some Vineyard people. Plus, Vineyard church plants have kept things in high gear, spreading Vineyard-style Christianity far and fast.

What makes this kind of Christianity unique?

- Music is front and center at Vineyard services.
- Expressions of the Spirit are cool. People don't have to worry about hiding the blessings of tongues, prophesying, healing, or whatever.
- Vineyard churches are only a *kind of* Pentecostal. They're not the same exact deal, and a lot of Vineyard members would say their kind of Christianity is more up with what's up today than Pentecostalism is.
- Small groups and home Bible studies are at the center of a lot of spiritual growth efforts at Vineyard churches.

Is there a statement of faith (SOF)?

Vineyard churches are in fellowship with one another, which means they each do their own thing but all basically stay on the same wavelength. You're not gonna find anything way out of whack from one church to the next when it comes to the SOF at a Vineyard church.

Following are some of the main ideas and Bible verses a Vineyard church might focus on:

- Satan is a real part of life and tries to bust in on God's rule to establish darkness, evil, and sin on earth: Revelation 12:7–9, Ephesians 6:12.
- Right when you get the Holy Spirit, you're baptized into the body of Christ. This baptism is what releases all the different spiritual gifts to people: Acts 2:1–4, 1 Corinthians 12:4–7.
- Five things are key for Vineyard Christianity:
  1. Worship,
  2. God's Word,
  3. Fellowship,
  4. Ministry, and
  5. Outreach.

Who's in charge?

Each Vineyard church has a pastor, or a few pastors, who are in charge of what's what at the church. There's not any one official guy in charge of everything that is Vineyard Christianity, so local church pastors are left to do their own thing.

Below pastors, you've got the different ministry leaders that help run things, like music, youth group, Sunday school, or other stuff like that.

What's the word for people my age?

Since each Vineyard community is its own deal, what you'll find just depends on who runs things for people your age.

But one cool thing is that Vineyard churches are very international. The Vineyard International Consortium (VIC) connects members across the globe: http://www.vineyard.org/. Then there's Planet Vineyard. It's a news and event listing site: http://www.mtit.com/mbvine/.

Another cool thing about Vineyard is music. Digital stuff like iTunes is online so you can download your favorite worship music all the time: http://www.vineyardmusicusa.com/usa/. And after you've downloaded what you're into, check out the Vineyard music festival, since it might be coming your way.

Is there anything going on besides church?

Vineyard churches are great at reaching out on a local level, like this Vineyard church does, offering social programs and support ministries: http://www.seattlevineyard.org/sunam/gettinginvolved.html.

Another thing going on has to do with publishing. Resources put out by Vineyard International Publishing (VIP) help pastors share their work and introduce non-Christians to ideas that reflect Vineyard beliefs and worship. So the publishing house ends up being a support system for Vineyard churches worldwide, but also a form of evangelism and ministry. The website for VIP is: http://www.vineyardbi.org/vip/About_Vip.htm.

How can I hook up with this kind of Christianity?

The main way to find out about Vineyard Christianity is to visit the VineyardUSA website: http://vineyardusa.org.

If you want more of a summary about Vineyard Christianity in general, try:
http://religiousmovements.lib.virginia.edu/nrms/Vineyard.html.

MAINLINE and MODERATE

SECTION

D

AFRICAN METHODIST EPISCOPAL

CHRISTIAN CHURCH
(Disciples of Christ)

CHRISTIAN METHODIST EPISCOPAL CHURCH

EPISCOPAL/ANGLICAN

FRIENDS (Quakers)

NATIONAL BAPTIST

THE PRESBYTERIAN CHURCH, USA

UNITED CHURCH OF CHRIST

UNITED METHODIST CHURCH

AFRICAN METHODIST EPISCOPAL

THE SHORT LIST

WHAT'S THE 1-2-3 RANK FOR THINGS TO FOCUS ON?

- Scripture
- Personal experience
- The traditions of African Methodist Christianity

WHAT'S THE BIBLE?

- The only book all Christians need in order to be saved and live a life of faith

WHAT'S THE CHURCH LIKE?

- Teamed up with others. Churches choose to cooperate with each other and keep the same values and beliefs.

WHOM DO I CONTACT?

- 1134 Eleventh St., NW, Washington, DC 20001
- Phone: (615) 256-5882
- URLs: http://www.amecnet.org/
  http://www.ame-church.com/

When did this kind of Christianity get started?

African Methodist Episcopal (AME) Christianity shares the same general history as Methodists but is something originally organized for African-American Methodists in particular. Methodists were the group who formed after taking the Protestant ideas about ways people could connect with Christianity taught by the Brethren and Pietist Movements and combining it with Minister John Wesley's set of principles—or methods—for living. That's where the name Methodist comes from. Methodist Christianity is all about using a certain rule, or method, for life.

In early America, Methodist Christianity was expanding and counted lots of African-Americans among its members. But this was back in like the 1700s when the majority of African-Americans were slaves. Some Christian groups didn't even let them worship alongside Caucasian Christians, but Methodists did. In fact, AME's founder, Richard Allen, preached to other African-Americans and was active in the ministry at a mixed-race church in Philadelphia. This doesn't mean Methodists were totally social rebels, though. Methodists believed in the equality of all people, but things inside the church weren't equal at all. There was segregation, and most African-Americans were treated like second-class citizens—they had different seating or meeting places and had to take Communion after Caucasian church members.

Richard Allen eventually had enough of all the segregation and going second in line and bolted. He loved God. He didn't love being discriminated against. Allen's idea was to start a church specifically for African-Americans. So after working with some other groups to get rolling, Allen branched out in his own direction, using his own money and land to set up shop. On April 9, 1794, Allen began preaching from Bethel African Church.

Bethel African was the first in a long line of AME churches founded over time. Today there's Allen's AME Church, and another large African-American group of Methodists that run the African Methodist Episcopal Zion

Church (AME Zion/AMEZ Church). They got going independently of Allen, but did so for a lot of the same reasons. Although Allen's AME church and the AME Zion group thought they'd hook up at one point, AME Zion decided to stay independent and became a whole other Christian group on its own.

The AME Zion group has got tons of members today, but Allen's AME Church has kept the more historical rep for being the first African-American Methodist church. (But be sure to check out the profile in this section for the Christian Methodist Episcopal Church (CME)—another African-American offshoot from Methodist Christianity.)

Have I heard of them before?

It depends. AME churches are way rooted in both American history and African-American history, but the church is usually better known among African-Americans than it is among other racial groups like Asians, Hispanics, or Caucasians.

What makes this kind of Christianity unique?

- AME beliefs and priorities are often summed up by the motto "God Our Father, Christ Our Redeemer, Man Our Brother."
- A person known as an Exhorter works as a kind of full-time mentor for AME members. Exhorters encourage others by sharing testimony. They also help explain and interpret Scripture and do things like teach, lead prayer, or organize small groups.
- Education is always on the books in terms of AME priorities. Church members founded the first private African-American college in America, Wilberforce University.

Is there a statement of faith (SOF)?

AME churches use the Apostles' Creed, but more importantly, they've got a list called the Twenty-five Articles of Religion that lay out the exact beliefs of AME Christians. And then besides these things there's something called *The Discipline,* a book full of stuff issued by AME founder Richard Allen that's been updated every year since the eighteenth century (1700s).

Following are some of the main ideas and Bible verses an AME church might focus on:

- Christian fellowship is a way to express God's love, and the church should welcome everyone unconditionally: 1 Thessalonians 3:12, Mark 9:38, 39.
- Living in Christ is the only way to walk as He walked. We're made right by our faith in Him, not by what we can accomplish on our own: John Wesley, Sermon 63.
- Conversion and repenting for our sins allow us to get past ourselves and into the confidence and mercy of God. That's what being born again is about: 1 John 5:1, John 3:8.

Who's in charge?

At the local level, AME churches—known as charges—have a few people looking over things. First, a presiding elder makes sure the local church is keeping things on track with AME beliefs and organization. But then you've got pastors who either do the local thing, staying put with a single AME church, or the itinerant thing, working at a single church for a year and then being reassigned as necessary.

At the top of everything, the AME runs a General Conference where church beliefs, doctrines, and other details are worked out and passed along to all AME churches. Everything gets decided on by vote, and people from all different levels of the church help make decisions, so it's an even-steven kind of thing.

What's the word for people my age?

AME churches have divisions of youth and of education that offer things like the Richard Allen Youth Council, but since each church is its own deal, what you'll find just depends on who runs things for people your age.

Almost for sure, though, you can hook up with a choir at an AME church. Music is a must-have during service, and with all the people who like to be involved in singing and music in most AME churches, a lot of communities have more than one choral group you can belong to, or have different choir styles. Some also offer dance, drama, or other kinds of creative outlets that'll tie faith and art together like this church does, shown online at: http://www.saintphilip.org/music&arts.htm.

Is there anything going on besides church?

AME churches go grass roots with efforts that impact local communities. A strong tradition of social activism has always been at the core of AME Christianity, so you'll always find programs centered on feeding the hungry or helping people find jobs at an AME church. Visit this website for a good example of the kinds of local ministries you'll find: http://209.238.123.84/FAME2003/index.html.

The Christian Recorder has been an AME standard since its first publication in 1848. It's got info from church leaders and news about who's in charge of what when it comes to the different AME churches across America: http://www.amecnet.org/Recorder/.

If you're thinking it'd be great to head to a Christian college, AME Christianity is at the core of a bunch of colleges: http://www.ame-today.com/abcsofame/higherlearning.shtml.

One last thing to keep an eye out for are the cultural things going on at AME churches that'll teach you more about what the AME Church has to do with African-American history or African culture in general.

How can I hook up with this kind of Christianity?

The main way to find out about AME Christianity is to visit three main websites:

- The African Methodist Episcopal Church: http://www.amecnet.org/
- The official website of the African Methodist Episcopal Church: http://www.amecnet.org/
- AME Today: http://www.ame-today.com/

If you want more of a summary about the AME Church in general, try: http://religiousmovements.lib.virginia.edu/nrms/ame.html.

CHRISTIAN CHURCH
(Disciples of Christ)

THE SHORT LIST

WHAT'S THE 1-2-3 RANK FOR THINGS TO FOCUS ON?

- The traditions of restorationist Christianity
- Scripture
- Personal experience

WHAT'S THE BIBLE?

- A guide that directs each person's conscience

WHAT'S THE CHURCH LIKE?

- Independent. There's no big central organization that runs all of the churches, but each sends representatives to regional and national assemblies.

WHOM DO I CONTACT?

- National Assembly
- 130 East Washington St., Indianapolis, IN 46204-3645
- Phone: (317) 635-3100; Fax (317) 635-3700
- URL: http://www.disciples.org

When did this kind of Christianity get started?

In America, the Disciples of Christ got started as one of the groups involved in a bigger movement called Restorationism (rest-oar-a-shun-is-um). The basic deal of this movement was unity, as outlined by the New Testament church. Different versions of Christianity were splitting believers into divided camps, all preaching that their kind of worship was right. Tired of all this division, people with restorationist ideas wanted to get Christians back together. Basically, it was a desire for a straightforward approach to Christian living that copied churches that came before, just as they were described in the New Testament.

One of the main guys preaching this message was Alexander Campbell. For him, independently run churches were the way to go. He saw no need for things like church creeds, different levels of leadership, and various kinds of church privileges, since he thought those things divided Christians. Campbell's ideas got popular, but like a lot of Christian groups that come on strong and get big membership numbers, Campbell's group of Christians eventually split into two sides. Campbell's Disciples of Christ became the more liberal and progressive group. The Churches of Christ became the conservative group. (Be sure to check out the profile for the Churches of Christ.) Since Campbell, the Disciples of Christ have been going strong. They've made a few changes here and there, like centralizing church government for official things. All in all, the Disciples of Christ are still centered on keeping things simple, uniting Christians, and giving local churches the freedom to run things on their own.

Have I heard of them before?

Probably so. With almost a million members, there's a good chance you know somebody who goes to a Disciples of Christ church. These churches are easy to get off the ground because of the importance Disciples of Christ Christianity puts on local churches. They're also very diverse on an ethnic level because of the importance placed on Christian unity.

What makes this kind of Christianity unique?

- Weekly worship includes the invitation—the chance to accept God.
- There's diversity on lots of ethnic levels, since Asian-Americans, or Hispanic-Americans, or African-Americans, or Caucasian-Americans run local Disciples of Christ churches. Some churches also ordain women and welcome homosexual Christians into the community.
- The Disciples of Christ are all about Christian unity. The Christian church shouldn't be split into lots of different groups.

Is there a statement of faith (SOF)?

The Disciples of Christ don't use official creeds and historical Christian statements of faith since the wording of such things has historically led to a lot of breakups and split-ups between Christians. Their only creed is Christ. Still, most Disciples of Christ Christians hold similar beliefs.

Following are some of the main ideas and Bible verses a Disciples of Christ community might focus on:

- Freedom of belief. Guided by the Bible, Christians can each follow their own conscience.
- Individual salvation isn't really individual. It's a group thing since you're being added to the larger Christian church: Acts 2:47.
- Baptism is key, but you have to be old enough to be able to express a desire for it, so no infant baptism.
- Christians need to witness, serve, and love as a way of sharing the Good News of Jesus Christ: Acts 1:8.

Who's in charge?

Local churches pick their own ministers (or pastors), make their own rules, handle their own money, and run all the day-to-day stuff.

Above the local church, there are boards that make planning- and direction-type decisions. At the tiptop of the organization, there is a general minister/president in charge of keeping everything on track in terms of general Disciples of Christ Christianity.

What's the word for people my age?

Since each Disciples of Christ church community is its own deal, what you'll find just depends on who runs things for people your age.

As for national connections, outreach ideas, conferences, retreats, and training programs you can find that online. The Disciples of Christ run a youth website at: http://www.homelandministries.org/YouthNews/main.html.

Is there anything going on besides church?

Missions and evangelism are key, but these are done through a variety of things that reach out on a local, community level, like AIDS ministries, racial and ethnic outreach programs, straight-up witnessing efforts, and social justice programs. Local missions programs like these are online at: http://www.homelandministries.org/index.htm.

Disciples of Christ churches believe in unity, meaning it's a regular thing for them to pair up with other kinds of charitable, religious, or social programs. Check out the following website link for the kinds of things going on: http://www.disciples.org/internal/resources/ecumenical.htm.

If you're thinking it'd be great to head to a Christian college, Disciples of Christ beliefs are at the core of a bunch of colleges. Check out these schools: http://www.dhedisciples.org/colleges/.

How can I hook up with this kind of Christianity?

The main way to find out about Disciples of Christ Christianity is to visit their main website: http://www.disciples.org/.

Use the "congregation finder" link if you like what you see to locate a church near you. Then give a look at the history of the church by heading over to the Disciples of Christ Historical Society: http://www.dishistsoc.org/.

CHRISTIAN METHODIST EPISCOPAL CHURCH

THE SHORT LIST

WHAT'S THE 1-2-3 RANK FOR THINGS TO FOCUS ON?

- Scripture
- Personal experience
- The traditions of the Christian Methodist Episcopal Church

WHAT'S THE BIBLE?

- Everything a Christian needs in order to be saved and live a life of faith compiled in one book

WHAT'S THE CHURCH LIKE?

- Teamed up with others. Churches cooperate with one another and keep the same values and beliefs.

WHOM DO I CONTACT?

- 4466 Elvis Presley Blvd., Memphis, TN 38116
- Phone: (205) 929-1640
- URL: http://www.c-m-e.org/

When did this kind of Christianity get started?

Christian Methodist Episcopal (CME) Christianity shares the same general history as Methodists, but grows into its own thing as a kind of Christianity organized for African-Americans. Methodist Christianity is all about using a certain rule, or method, for life. That's where the name Methodist comes from. Methodists were the group who formed after taking the Protestant ideas about ways people could connect with Christianity taught by the Brethren and Pietist Movements and combining it with Minister John Wesley's set of principles—or methods—for living.

In early America, Methodist Christianity was expanding and counted many African-Americans among its members. And here we're talking early America, like during the 1700s early. So at this time the majority of African-Americans were slaves. Lots of Christian groups didn't even let African-Americans worship alongside Caucasian Christians, but Methodists were one group that did. There was still a lot of segregation and racism and discrimination in the church, though. African-Americans were definitely not treated as equals, even if Methodists were letting them come to the same worship services. So it's no surprise that as soon as African-American slaves were emancipated after the Civil War, they wanted to do their own thing. They wanted an independent kind of Methodism where they didn't have to deal with all the racial fallout that caused friction in Caucasian Methodist churches.

The break from Methodism started when a group of known leaders in the African-American community organized a branch of the faith that still did the Methodist thing in terms of belief but had a separate place to worship more geared to African-Americans on the whole. The Methodists these African-Americans had been worshiping with in the past weren't too thrilled but finally agreed to let them do their own thing, as blacks had been emancipated from slavery and many freed slaves wanted to belong to and control their own church. The two Methodist groups split ways, and since then the African-American group has been known as the Christian Methodist Episcopal Church (CME). Today the CME Church is still its own deal, and is one of three main kinds of Christianity started by African-American Methodists, but it's the one most directly associated with the move out of slavery and into freedom.

Have I heard of them before?

It depends. CME churches have tons of members but are usually better known among African-Americans than they are among other racial groups like Asians, Hispanics, or Caucasians.

What makes this kind of Christianity unique?

- The CME Church's history as an independent religious organization for African-Americans translates into big attention on supporting, developing, and offering spiritual teaching to African-Americans.
- African culture and heritage combine with Methodist Christianity at some CME churches, creating new kinds of worship and celebration.
- CME communities are okay with women being ordained as pastors.
- A person known as an Exhorter works as a kind of full-time mentor for CME members. Exhorters encourage others by sharing testimony, helping to explain and interpret Scripture, and they also do things like teach, lead prayer, or organize small groups.

Is there a statement of faith (SOF)?

CME churches use the Nicene Creed, the Apostles' Creed, and also have a list called the Twenty-five Articles of Religion. The Articles lay out the exact beliefs CME Christians hold.

Following are some of the main ideas and Bible verses a Christian Methodist Episcopal Church might focus on:

- God desires Christians to care for the physical well-being of other people and also commit to finding ways for those in need to access housing, food, employment, or education.
- Living in Christ is the only way to walk as He walked. We're made right by our faith in Him, not by what we can accomplish on our own: John Wesley, Sermon 63.
- Conversion and repentance for our sins allow us to get past ourselves and into the confidence and mercy of God. That's what being born again is about: 1 John 5:1, John 3:8.

Who's in charge?

A bishop presides over each group of local churches. That's the Episcopal thing in the CME church name. But on the local level, pastors run CME churches. They can be guys or girls, but they have to be licensed to preach by the CME Church.

At the top of CME Christianity, there is the General Conference. It's a place where representatives from different CME churches gather to decide on the official stuff for the year for all CME communities, making CME Christianity an even-steven kind of deal.

What's the word for people my age?

CME churches have divisions of youth and of education that might offer different outlets and events you can tie yourself into, but since each church is its own deal, what you'll find just depends on who runs things for people your age.

On a national level, though, you can get with other CME members through the Connectional Youth and Young Adult Conference, or CYAAC:
http://www.c-m-e.org/2004%20Y&YA%20Conf%20Update.htm.

Is there anything going on besides church?

CME churches go grass roots with a lot of their outreach, supporting things like hospitals and housing complexes for the elderly or for low-income families. Programs make direct impacts in the neighborhoods around local CME churches, like these ministries shown at:
http://russellmemorial.com/ministry.htm.

The publishing arm of the CME Church puts out various materials you can look through at:
http://www.cmepublishinghouse.com/.

And then there's *The Christian Index*, which is the official publication of the CME Church: http://www.c-m-e.org/core/Christian%20Index%20Opening%20Page.htm.

If you're thinking it'd be great to head to a Christian college, CME Christianity is at the core of a bunch of colleges: http://www.c-m-e.org/core/higher_learning.htm.

Also, be sure to keep up with cultural things going on at local CME churches that'll teach you more about what CME Christianity has to do with African-American history or African culture in general.

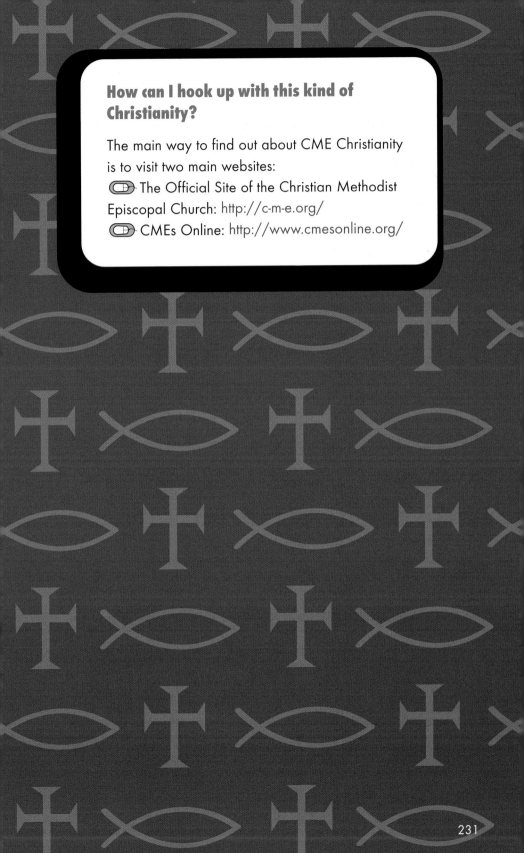

How can I hook up with this kind of Christianity?

The main way to find out about CME Christianity is to visit two main websites:

- The Official Site of the Christian Methodist Episcopal Church: http://c-m-e.org/
- CMEs Online: http://www.cmesonline.org/

EPISCOPAL/ANGLICAN
The Episcopal Church

WHAT'S THE 1-2-3 RANK FOR THINGS TO FOCUS ON?

- The traditions of Episcopal/Anglican Christianity
- The experience you get from the sacraments (rituals)
- Scripture

WHAT'S THE BIBLE?

- A Christian's primary guide for living that doesn't always have to be read the same way by every Christian

WHAT'S THE CHURCH LIKE?

- Teamed up with others. Churches choose to cooperate with each other and keep the same values and beliefs.

WHOM DO I CONTACT?

- 815 Second Ave., New York, NY 10017
- Phone: (800) 334-7626
- URL: http://ecusa.anglican.org/

When did this kind of Christianity get started?

Before we get into how Episcopal Christians became a group, there's a fact that's essential to getting the bigger picture of what's going on with the Episcopal Church. See, it's the American version of the Anglican Church (the official

Church of England), which means there's a good chance you'll hear Episcopal Christians talking about Anglican this or Anglican that. We'll get into how the two churches are related, but right up front it's good to know how Episcopal Christianity fits in with Anglican Christianity since you hear the names of these two kinds of Christianity together a lot.

So you had Martin Luther preaching new ideas about Christianity in Europe during the Middle Ages, and that's the info that flowed over to England and inspired people to eventually follow Luther's lead. The Church of England (COE) wanted to go Luther's direction in terms of interpreting the Bible and breaking away from the Pope and the Catholic Church, but there was a snag in the plan since one of Luther's ideas didn't really support the formal worship style and all the rituals the COE liked to use in services. So in the end, the COE basically split the difference between Luther and the Catholic Church. Luther's ideas about the Bible and the ways Christians relate to God were in, but so were the traditional forms of worship Catholics used. It was a combo deal, or a balance of the two, that became known as Anglican Christianity, or Anglicanism.

Anglican and Episcopal Christianity are basically the same deal, just set up in two different locations. Anglican Christianity is in England. Episcopal Christianity is an American thing. Anglican Christianity did make a brief appearance on the American scene, but this was back before the American Revolution and, well, you can imagine what success a church might have trying to establish itself by saying: "Hey, guess what, you bunch of people trying to liberate yourselves from the British! We're the official Church of England; how cool is that?! Want to come to our 'Get to Know Us' member night?!"

Pretty much the answer was no. People in the colonies were trying to boot the English out, and the American Revolution was all about establishing the colonies as a separate, independent place where England didn't have control over government or religion. What all that means is that it was basically a no-go for Anglicanism. And that's where Episcopal Christianity comes in. It's an American version of Anglicanism that's totally, completely its own dec and was established through two general councils between 1785 and 1789.

Have I heard of them before?

Almost for sure. Episcopal Christianity got its official start in America just about the same time America actually became America. Both things were results of the American Revolution, so Episcopal Christians have had a long time to spread out and establish things.

The Episcopal Church is also well known in twenty-first-century America for the decision made by church members in 2003 to elect a homosexual man to the position of church bishop, which meant the guy would be in a leadership position over a bunch of local churches. Some Episcopal and Anglican Christians hit the roof when they heard the news, but the reactions were different all over the world. As of 2005, nothing's been resolved and the debates, disagreements, and discussions continue to make news headlines.

What makes this kind of Christianity unique?

- There are *high* and *low* Episcopal churches. High churches are way formal and get really into ritual. Low churches are still formal, but in a laid-back way compared to high Episcopal churches.
- Churches have mostly the same rituals and services but can be totally different in their biblical beliefs. Interpretations run from ultraliberal to pretty conservative, but everyone is still considered an Episcopal Christian.
- The Book of Common Prayer contains the entire collection of worship services used in Episcopal Christianity. Everybody uses the Book of Common Prayer each week, on the same schedule.
- Episcopal Christians are okay with women being ordained as deacons, pastors, or bishops.

Is there a statement of faith (SOF)?

The church does the historical thing, using the Nicene and Apostles' Creeds. They also use something called the Thirty-nine Articles of Religion, sometimes called the Thirty-nine Articles of the Church of England.

Following are some of the main ideas and Bible verses an Episcopal Christian church might focus on:

- The core of Christianity is a commitment to Christ's teachings, but they should be made fresh so the Gospel can be known to new generations: Hebrews 10:23.
- Our ability to think critically, to reason, and to question things is a complement to Scripture. It's part of God's call to live a full and healthy Christian life.
- Dialogue with people of other faiths is part of the Christian life. It begins with mutual understanding, respect, trust, and being dedicated to service and community efforts as witnesses for Christ.

Who's in charge?

On a local level the minister (priest) leads most things. But the reason Episcopal Christians are called Episcopal is because the word actually means bishop, so that's who's basically in charge of different Episcopal church communities—bishops.

Episcopal and Anglican churches also stay in touch with the Anglican Communion, a big group churches can choose to belong to that holds meetings and conventions and pins down any big changes in ideas or beliefs.

What's the word for people my age?

Churches are organized into local and regional groups, so you can check your area for things going on there, but then on a national level be sure to check out the Episcopal Youth Event (EYE) next time you're online: http://www.eye2005.org.

Is there anything going on besides church?

Episcopal churches get into lots of outreach efforts based on social issues. A good example of the kinds of things going on are letter-writing campaigns, political-type stuff, or peace and justice ministries that work locally as a support system for other groups in need of some extra help. Check it out:

CD Peace and Justice Ministries:
http://ecusa.anglican.org/peace_justice.htm

CD The Episcopal Public Policy Network:
http://ecusa.anglican.org/eppn.htm

Creative ways of promoting spiritual development are also something very Episcopal. The kinds of things happening on that front can be found at the website:
http://ecusa.anglican.org/20966_ENG_HTM.htm?menupage=11761.

If you're thinking it might be great to head to a Christian college, there's a website that offers student exchanges and other ways to learn about Episcopal Christianity on campus before you make any big decisions about where you're heading: http://www.cuac.org/.

How can I hook up with this kind of Christianity?

The main way to find out about Episcopal Christianity is to visit their main website, using the link set up for "seekers": http://ecusa.anglican.org/index_flash.htm.

You can also click over to the Anglican Communion website, since that'll fill in the blanks a little bit in terms of the bigger, worldwide group Episcopal and Anglican Christians form together: http://www.anglicancommunion.org/index.cfm.

FRIENDS (Quakers)

THE SHORT LIST

WHAT'S THE 1-2-3 RANK FOR THINGS TO FOCUS ON?

- Personal experience you get from the Inner Light of Christ
- The traditions of Quaker Christianity
- Scripture

WHAT'S THE BIBLE?

- A valuable guide Christians can use in combo with individual guidance received from the Spirit of God

WHAT'S THE CHURCH LIKE?

- Teamed up with others. Churches choose to cooperate with one another and keep the same values and beliefs.

WHOM DO I CONTACT?

- 1216 Arch St., #2B, Philadelphia, PA 19107
- Phone: (317) 635-3100; Fax (317) 635-3700
- URL: http://fgcquaker.org/

When did this kind of Christianity get started?

The Friends are a British import to America started when a guy named George Fox began to search for more spiritual clarity in his life. The Friends' history has it that Fox wandered all over England and spent years on this search, trying to sort out his personal beliefs to find something real. It was tough, though. Fox was tempted by this and that, and a lot of his searches turned up nothing, which began to bum him out. He'd seriously been asking everyone and doing everything he could think of to get the clarity he was after. He searched the Scriptures. He got help from priests. He asked other believers what was up in their lives. Fox even asked people who didn't believe in God what was going on for them, and why they didn't find their home in Christ. But in the end, Fox ended up with nothing. He just didn't find the authentic faith he was looking for in the Christian churches of his day, or in the kind of worship he saw others taking part in.

And then it finally happened. Fox got the clarity he was after. It wasn't because of his searching, though; it was because of God. Fox is said to have experienced a revelation. It was like an overwhelmingly personal connection that was direct and clear. The connection became something Fox started calling the Inner Light or Inner Voice, and he preached that all Christians could have it. Fox based this idea on his own experience, saying the voice he'd heard told him about the Inner Light and that it was all based on John 1:9. In the kind of Bible Fox would have been reading at the time (King James Version), the verse said: "That was the true Light, which lighteth every man that cometh into the world."

Fox preached his ideas and eventually people who listened found that he was right. By following his teachings, they experienced the Inner Light for themselves. Some stories say the Inner Light was so overwhelming it caused people to shake and tremble when it happened to them. They quaked, people said. And in time the Friends picked up the nickname Quakers because of these reports.

So Friends Christianity took off in England through the teachings of Fox and then hit the shores of America during colonial times. It was hard for Friends communities to get a fair chance at first. Fox taught that people could be in charge of their own spirituality and their own churches, which was so not okay at that time. But the Friends remained strong and continued to grow little bits at a time, until they totally scored when one of their members, William Penn, was granted the colony of Pennsylvania. The whole thing was his, and so in 1681 Penn's like, "Hey! Move it on over to Pennsylvania."

Today, Friends Christianity hasn't grown into anything too huge. The group is still on the small side in comparison to other kinds of Christianity, but they've definitely had a lasting impact and are still on the scene.

Have I heard of them before?

It depends. Friends aren't big promoters, their communities aren't large, and they don't have any famous pastors or basically do anything that could make them high-profile. They do evangelize, though, and contribute to lots of social outreach ministries. So it's not like you wouldn't ever run into Friends Christians; it's just that they're not out there doing things in a flashy way.

What makes this kind of Christianity unique?

- Friends services are called meetings, and there are two kinds. One is programmed, and has a minister, a sermon, etc. . . . The other is unprogrammed, and is silent. Anyone there is welcome to speak if they feel led by the Spirit to say something.
- There's no Communion (Lord's Supper/Eucharist) at a Friends meeting.
- Men and women are completely equal, and either sex can lead, speak, minister, or direct a Friends community.
- Friends worship God by serving Him through society. Outreach ministries and peace and justice ministries are a major focus in Friends communities.

Is there a statement of faith (SOF)?

Friends stick by their statement that "the Spirit of Christ, which leads us into all Truth, will never move us to fight and war against any man with outward weapons, neither for the kingdom of Christ, nor for the kingdoms of this world" (Declaration from Quakers to King Charles II, 1660).

Following are some of the main ideas and Bible verses a Friends community might focus on:

- God can be received directly, by anybody, at anytime. Outward ceremonies and rituals can't take the place of an inner relationship with God.
- The best way to defeat injustice, war, and other negativity in the world is to look within and untangle ourselves from our role in these things: Romans 12:21.
- Original sin is out, and the inherent goodness of human beings is in. Perfection and freedom from sin are possible in this life.

Who's in charge?

Honestly, everybody is. Everyone's a minister in a Friends community. But to get specific, each Friends community runs itself and considers everyone in the community equally in charge. It's a completely even-steven thing.

What's the word for people my age?

Since each Friends community is its own deal, what you'll find just depends on who runs things for people your age.

On a national level, there's YSOP (the Youth Service Opportunities Project). It's a social outreach program you can read up on at this website:
http://www.ysop.org/home.htm.

There's also a national conference set up for Quakers called YouthQuake:
http://www.youthquake.org/.

You can also go online to keep up with international discussion lists and to get more info on regional Friends communities:
http://www.quaker.org/#9.

Is there anything going on besides church?

Social justice and the promotion of nonviolence are two of the biggest things going on in Friends communities. Ministries to get involved with are pretty endless, as Friends are doing everything from working on national political stuff to traveling across the globe to helping with international relief efforts. Following are a few outreach programs that'll give you an idea what Friends are doing:

- Quaker Earthcare Witness: http://www.fcun.org/
- Alternatives to Violence Project: http://www.avpusa.org/
- Right Sharing of World Resources: http://www.rswr.org/
- Friends for a Non-Violent World: http://www.fnvw.org/

If you're thinking it'd be great to head to a Christian college, Friends Christianity is at the core of a bunch of schools: http://www.quaker.org/colleges.html.

How can I hook up with this kind of Christianity?

There are a few different big groups of Friends communities today, so it's best to have a look at them all and then use the Friends locator link to get hooked up with something near you.

- Friends General Conference: http://fgcquaker.org/
- Friends United Meeting: http://www.fum.org/
- Evangelical Friends International: http://www.evangelical-friends.org/
- Friends locator: http://www.quakerfinder.org/

If you want more of a summary about the Friends in general try: http://religiousmovements.lib.virginia.edu/nrms/quak.html.

NATIONAL BAPTIST
National Baptist Convention, USA, Inc.

THE SHORT LIST

WHAT'S THE 1-2-3 RANK FOR THINGS TO FOCUS ON?

- Scripture
- Personal experience
- The traditions of Baptist Christianity

WHAT'S THE BIBLE?

- A perfect treasure of heavenly instruction full of principles that are the supreme standard for living

WHAT'S THE CHURCH LIKE?

- Teamed up with others. Churches choose to cooperate with one another and keep the same values and beliefs.

WHOM DO I CONTACT?

- 1700 Baptist World Center Dr., Nashville, TN 37207
- Phone: (615) 228-6292
- URL: http://www.nationalbaptist.com/

When did this kind of Christianity get started?

After separating from the church they'd been going to in England, John Smyth and Thomas Helwys started to focus on two things they thought should be central in their faith: the idea that God's grace was something for everyone and a belief in adult baptism. The baptism thing is where Baptist Christians get their name, since baptism was seen as a necessity for all Christians who worshiped in this way.

Smyth and Helwys were from England, but by the 1600s their ideas were in America. On the East Coast, Baptists were making the scene and picking up new believers, but almost right from the start African-American Baptists weren't able to do their own thing. Because of slavery, prejudice, and racism, black Baptists had to play backup to white Baptists. Though there were a few independent black Baptist churches established, they had to belong to bigger Baptist associations run by whites, which meant the issues important to African-Americans weren't up at the top of the priority list. This all changed with the signing of the Emancipation Proclamation in 1863 and the Thirteenth Amendment to the U.S. Constitution in 1865. Slavery was ended, leading to black Baptists "getting" regional churches together and forming various church conventions made up of Baptist Christians in the late 1800s.

As regional groups came together, a national group for black Baptists was born, known as the National Baptist Convention. Today it's known as the National Baptist Convention, USA, Inc. (NBCUSA). Like lots of Christian groups, they ended up splitting into different groups like the National Baptist Convention of America (NBCA) and the Progressive National Baptist Convention (PNBC). Even with the splits, though, most black Baptists stayed true to the core things Smyth and Helwys cared about at the beginning of Baptist Christianity. Adult baptism was still key and so was evangelism.

Today the National Baptist Convention, USA, Inc. (NBCUSA) is the largest group of black Baptists in America. Because of the dilemmas they faced due to racial restrictions and other forms of legal injustice, NBCUSA churches promote a kind of Christianity that works for justice and equality for all people. They are tied to specific movements for African-Americans, such as civil rights.

But the big undercurrent behind a lot of Baptist growth for NBCUSA was tied to the publishing board they set up. It was key in circulating African-American sermons, Sunday school materials, and other writings about black Christianity. This really grounded the NBCUSA and helped it grow. Since then, this kind of Christianity has stayed solid on the scene through their combo of Smyth-and-Helwys-inspired Baptist beliefs and a desire for racial equality and independence.

Have I heard of them before?

It depends. The NBCUSA is definitely big-time in terms of membership, but it's better known among African-Americans than it usually is among other racial groups like Asians, Hispanics, or Caucasians.

What makes this kind of Christianity unique?

- NBCUSA churches choose to belong.
- Together, all the NBCUSA churches combine to form the largest group of black Baptists in America.
- The NBCUSA president speaks out on social and biblical issues. He's really involved and high-profile.
- NBCUSA churches practice adult baptism with total immersion, which means you've got to be old enough to make your own choice to be baptized, and you've gotta get all the way dunked when it happens.

Is there a statement of faith (SOF)?

NBCUSA member churches use the Articles of Faith. You can read these at http://www.nationalbaptist.com/images/documents/26.pdf. Besides the Articles of Faith, the NBCUSA puts out Position Statements every so often that list ideas and causes National Baptists should get behind.

Following are some of the main ideas and Bible verses a NBCUSA church community might focus on:

- People need to hear God's Word through home and foreign missions: Isaiah 55.
- Vision, integrity, structure, and accountability (V.I.S.A.) are the qualities National Baptist Christians aim to live out.
- Church and state should be separate, but it's the duty of Christians to support their government leaders as long as they don't go against the will of God: Acts 4:19–20, Romans 13:1–7.

Who's in charge?

Each NBCUSA church is its own deal and takes care of itself. But there are standards of belief when it comes to being included as a member church. These beliefs and general decisions about where NBCUSA Christianity is going are worked out at the yearly gathering, headed by the NBCUSA president.

Local church leadership is directed by a pastor. Other leadership positions—like bishop or deacon—are available, but NBCUSA churches believe only a specific number of leadership positions can be found in the New Testament books of Timothy and Titus, so people can work only in those roles.

What's the word for people my age?

Since each NBCUSA church community is its own deal, what you'll find just depends on who runs things for people your age.

Is there anything going on besides church?

Publishing, missions, and education are the main priorities for the NBCUSA. On the publishing side, magazines like the *National Baptist Voice* (http://www.nationalbaptist.com/Index.cfm?FuseAction=Page&PageID=1000101) and the *E & E Connection* (http://www.nationalbaptist.com/Index.cfm?FuseAction=Page&PageID=1000328) get the word out about things going on in general around the NBCUSA. And then on top of that there's the NBCUSA Sunday school publishing board catalog for lessons, ideas, educational resources, and stuff like that: (http://www.nationalbaptist.com/index.cfm?FuseAction=Page&PageID=1000000).

Three main boards do most of the mission work: the evangelism board, the home missions board, and the foreign missions board. You can read about each online at http://www.nationalbaptist.com/Index.cfm?FuseAction=Page&PageID=1000019.

If you're thinking it'd be great to head to a Christian college, NBCUSA beliefs are at the core of American Baptist College, and you can read up on that school at http://www.abcnash.edu/.

How can I hook up with this kind of Christianity?

The main way to find out about NBCUSA Christianity is to visit their main website: http://www.nationalbaptist.com/Index.cfm ?FuseAction=Page&PageID=1000311.

Also, be sure to visit the other two National Baptist Christian groups:

◉ National Baptist Convention of America, Inc. (NBCA): http://www.nbcamerica.net

◉ Progressive National Baptist Convention (PNBC): http://www.pnbc.demo.nurevelation.com/home.aspx

THE PRESBYTERIAN CHURCH, USA

THE SHORT LIST

WHAT'S THE 1-2-3 RANK FOR THINGS TO FOCUS ON?

- Scripture
- The traditions of Calvinist theology
- Personal experience

WHAT'S THE BIBLE?

- An authoritative book for living that can be understood by each person's own conscience—since it's directed by God

WHAT'S THE CHURCH LIKE?

- Teamed up with others. Churches choose to cooperate with one another and keep the same values and beliefs.

WHOM DO I CONTACT?

- 100 Witherspoon St., Louisville, KY 40202-1396
- Phone: (800) 872-3283
- URL: http://www.pcusa.org/

When did this kind of Christianity get started?

Presbyterians came up from a set of beliefs influenced by a guy living during the time of Martin Luther named John Calvin. They're known for the influence of his ideas in Presbyterian teaching, but they're also known for using a kind of church organization that promotes an even-steven kind of leadership shared between ministers and church members.

John Calvin was a French/Swiss theologian. After looking at what Luther had to say, Calvin took to it and eventually reached enough people with his ideas that a whole movement started. The main thing Calvin wanted Christians to emphasize in their faith was God's ultimate rule over the world and over people's lives. This emphasis led people to get really into their responsibilities as humans. Learning, understanding God's Word, and working together to reach these goals was key.

People after Calvin continued to teach his emphasis on God's ultimate rule, the most famous of these people being a guy named John Knox. Knox studied with Calvin and took his teachings back to Scotland. But even without Knox, Calvin-style Christianity was taking off, and that's what would lay the foundations for the kind of Christianity we now call Presbyterianism.

In America, Presbyterianism got rolling in the 1700s when European immigrants arrived in the States. In 1706, descendants of the Puritans met up with Scottish Presbyterians who had come to America, and they made the group a formal deal a little bit later. By 1788, the group was an independent Presbyterian church.

Just like they'd been doing in Europe, Presbyterians organized things around the presbytery, a group of local churches all working together. They also set up the government so it was in the hands of regular people known as presbyters. They'd get elected, ordained as elders, and then be all set to help guide things for the church. It was pretty unique when this whole system started since it meant people had tons of control over their own church's affairs, spiritual growth, and the training of new Presbyterian ministers.

Over the years there were definitely some breaks between liberal and conservative Presbyterians, but that didn't keep some of the bigger groups from coming together. The Presbyterian Church, USA (PCUSA) is one of these big groups.

Have I heard of them before?

Maybe. Presbyterian Christianity has been around in America for a long time, which means it's had a lot of time to show up on the scene, get some attention, and grow.

Also, Presbyterians have a lock on being the trendsetters in terms of getting regular worshipers involved in church organization and government, so even if you haven't heard about Presbyterian Christianity, you may go to a church influenced by Presbyterian-style organization.

What makes this kind of Christianity unique?

- Organizing and directing church stuff is always done through a combo of leaders and laypeople.
- PCUSA churches are okay with women being ordained ministers and leading churches.
- Presbyterians are serious about taking God seriously. God's majesty, holiness, and ultimate rule are a big part of Presbyterian beliefs.
- There are liberal and conservative Presbyterians, which means biblical interpretations can be way different from church to church, even though everyone's still considered a Presbyterian.

Is there a statement of faith (SOF)?

The PCUSA uses the Brief Statement of Faith. Overall, though, the bulk of what's believed by Presbyterian Christians is found in the Book of Confessions, which has more historical stuff in it like the Nicene Creed, the Apostles' Creed, and Presbyterian-specific statements like the Westminster Confession of Faith.

Following are some of the main ideas and Bible verses a Presbyterian community might focus on:

- Christians can't be indifferent to the evils in the world and need to speak out against the social and moral issues that are breaking things down.
- The Holy Spirit is what allows Christians to grow in faith and gives believers the will to become like God: John 16:13.
- Sin is a condition of the heart. It expresses how far away from God we are, and only God can make us realize this: Romans 3:23.

Who's in charge?

At the tiptop of the PCUSA, you've got a General Assembly. It's a place where representatives from different PCUSA communities get together and decide on all the official stuff that's going to be nailed down for the year.

At the local level, each PCUSA community runs itself using a minister (pastor) and a group of other church members who've been elected. The perspectives of church leaders and regular community members are all represented. It's an even-steven kind of deal.

What's the word for people my age?

Since each PCUSA community is its own deal, what you'll find just depends on who runs things for people your age, but on the national level you've got the Presbyterian Youth Connection (PYC) running retreats, conferences, and that kind of thing: http://www.pcusa.org/youthministry/.

You'll also want to check out the Youth Ministry & Spirituality Project (YMSP). It's a program thought up at one of the PCUSA schools in California and pushes to get a bigger group of young Christians to hook up, even if they practice different kinds of Christianity: http://www.ymsp.org/.

Is there anything going on besides church?

First, it's important to know how ecumenical PCUSA churches run. Even if everybody doesn't agree on each and every point of Christian doctrine, PCUSA Christians are willing to work with other believers to get things done. Unity is more important than being right. Following is the list of other kinds of Christians the PCUSA works with:

http://www.pcusa.org/links/international.htm.

Second, PCUSA churches do the missions and outreach thing and have a website that allows you to read about everything they're doing from local to world to national outreach: http://www.pcusa.org/navigation/mission.htm.

Third, if you're thinking it'd be great to head to a Christian college, Presbyterian Christianity is at the core of a bunch of colleges. Check out these schools:

http://www.pcusa.org/colleges/index.htm.

How can I hook up with this kind of Christianity?

The main way to find out about PCUSA Christianity is to visit their main website and then use the "find a church" link on the front page to locate a church near you: http://www.pcusa.org/.

UNITED CHURCH OF CHRIST

THE SHORT LIST

WHAT'S THE 1-2-3 RANK FOR THINGS TO FOCUS ON?

- The traditions of Christianity
- Scripture
- Personal experience

WHAT'S THE BIBLE?

- A witness of God's overall message that can offer up new info with each passing generation

WHAT'S THE CHURCH LIKE?

- Teamed up with others. Churches choose to cooperate with one another and keep the same values and beliefs.

WHOM DO I CONTACT?

- 700 Prospect Ave., Cleveland, OH 44115
- Phone: (866) 822-8224
- URL: http://www.ucc.org/

When did this kind of Christianity get started?

If any kind of Christianity blends elements of other churches, it's the United Church of Christ (UCC). This kind of Christianity is Protestant, meaning that people in UCC communities understand a person's relationship to God in a way that goes back to the Middle Ages and to a Catholic monk named Martin Luther. He encouraged Christians to believe in and follow nothing more and nothing less than what was written in the Bible, but didn't think this was going on in Catholic Christianity. So by the time Luther laid out all his interpretations and ideas, it added up to an altogether different kind of Christianity from Catholicism. Today we know Luther's ideas as Protestant Christianity. UCC Christianity comes up from this history.

The UCC got its start in America when one group, then another, then another, and then another all joined forces into a kind of megadiverse Christianity. Kinds of Christianity that had been going since colonial times all came together in the late 1950s, and that's how the UCC was born. There were Reform Christians coming to the table with their particular Christian ideas from places in Europe like Germany and Switzerland. You had Congregational Christians coming to the table with Pilgrim- and Puritan-era beliefs in independent church communities. You had Evangelical Christians coming to the table with their emphasis on working with other Christian groups through the message of the Gospel.

And then you had Christian Christians. Yeah, that's right . . . Christian Christians. They came to the table talking about returning to the simplicity of early Christianity. (Check out the profiles in the **EVANGELICAL and CONSERVATIVE** and **MAINLINE and MODERATE** sections for the Churches of Christ and the Disciples of Christ, two kinds of Christianity that got their start in this bigger group of Christian Christians.)

This was back in the 1950s. When the four groups came together, they did so with the idea that freedom of belief would play a big role in the UCC. With such diverse kinds of Christianity all coming together, freedom had to be a priority, since the four groups weren't going to all agree on every little point. This meant that future UCC churches were given a lot of breathing room. A shared faith in Jesus and an emphasis on Christian unity were key. What someone thought about a particular verse or what official church creed someone used wasn't that big a deal. That kind of stuff was secondary.

UCC ideas about the freedom of belief and also how united the UCC understands all believers to be since Jesus is their focal point were two ideas right off the bat. It was a popular idea among Christian churches. The UCC was already kinda big when it started, since it was made up from four groups of Christians that already existed. But the emphasis on uniting Christians despite their differences gave the UCC a big space in which to grow, and it hasn't stopped expanding. Since the group formed back in the 1950s, it has picked up members and stayed true to the Christian diversity at its core.

Have I heard of them before?

Maybe. UCC churches come in almost every shape, size, style of belief, and way of worship, but they're mostly on the liberal side of Christianity. This means Christians in conservative circles may have never heard about UCC Christianity, or haven't heard very good things about it. That said, UCC Christians keep on trying to unite believers, so you may have run into a UCC Christian involved in, say, a local service project or a world evangelism mission—even if some other kind of Christian group was sponsoring the event.

What makes this kind of Christianity unique?

- UCC communities can be totally different in their biblical beliefs—liberal, not, whatever.
- UCC churches ordain people called to serve. It doesn't matter if they're male, female, homosexual, heterosexual.
- Working with other kinds of Christian groups toward overall Christian unity is more important than proving that UCC beliefs and interpretations are right or best.
- Most UCC church services go traditional, using a Book of Worship, Bible readings set to a yearly calendar, and lots of seasonal rituals.

Is there a statement of faith (SOF)?

An original version of the UCC statement of faith is online here: http://www.ucc.org/faith/faith.htm. Then you've also got all the confessions, creeds, and beliefs of the four churches that got UCC rolling in the first place: http://www.ucc.org/faith/index.html.

Following are some of the main ideas and Bible verses a UCC community might focus on:

- Christianity comes with the responsibility to act in love and justice: Micah 6:8, Matthew 23:37–39.
- Certain aspects of Christianity are essential, like unity in God. Other aspects aren't, so why divide believers? Christians are free to form their own views on the nonessentials, such as how a person interprets certain biblical passages, chooses to organize their life, or decides to worship: John 17:21.
- Today's church continues to show what the apostles showed—that Christ is real and powerful.
- Baptism is for everyone—babies, kids, grandparents, and so forth: Acts 2:38, Galatians 3:26–28.

Who's in charge?

At the top of the UCC churches a general minister/president acts as a spiritual leader keeping everything on track, but not laying down biblical interpretations or hard rules every partner church has to follow.

Local UCC churches take care of things on their own for the most part. Churches in the same area choose to belong to associations in order to work together, but not everybody has to decide all the same things or have the exact same beliefs.

What's the word for people my age?

Since each UCC community is its own deal, what you'll
find just depends on who runs things for people your age.

In terms of national UCC youth stuff, there's a general
website with sermons, opportunities to travel with your faith
through global pilgrimages, info for the yearly UCC youth
conference, and ways to get more into spiritual
development: http://www.ucc.org/youth/index.html.

Is there anything going on besides church?

Outreach at most UCC churches is centered on making a
difference in various social issues, like antiwar efforts or
ways to create fair and equitable social standards for all
human beings. All the kinds of things going on are on the
website: http://www.ucc.org/justice/index.html. Or you
can check out this link to read about the other volunteer
ministries going on:
http://www.ucc.org/ministries/volunteer/index.html.

If you're thinking it'd be great to head to a Christian
college, UCC Christianity is at the core of a bunch of
schools: http://www.ucc.org/education/school/index.html.

How can I hook up with this kind of Christianity?

The main way to find out about UCC Christianity is to
visit their main website and then use the "find a church"
link if you like what you see:
http://www.ucc.org/index3.html.

UNITED METHODIST CHURCH

THE SHORT LIST

WHAT'S THE 1-2-3 RANK FOR THINGS TO FOCUS ON?

- The methods for living taught by the Wesleyan tradition
- Scripture
- Personal experience

WHAT'S THE BIBLE?

- The primary source for Christian doctrine that people can use their own minds to interpret and ask questions about

WHAT'S THE CHURCH LIKE?

- Teamed up with others. Churches cooperate with one another and keep the same values and beliefs.

WHOM DO I CONTACT?

- P.O. Box 320, 810 Twelfth Ave. S., Nashville, TN 37202-0320
- Phone: (800) 251-8140
- URL: http://www.umc.org/

When did this kind of Christianity get started?

Methodist Christianity came up by shooting off from the Protestant Movement known as the Brethren, or Pietist Movement. A guy named Jacob Spener liked Martin Luther's ideas but wanted to put a twist on them by shaking up the ways people heard God's Word. He wanted it to touch people in their hearts, not just their minds. So the Brethren and Pietists used things like minichurch or small group study, Sunday school, youth fellowship, and other stuff like women's groups to get people worshiping together in more tight-knit ways then just all showing up at the same weekly service.

The main leaders of Methodism—John and Charles Wesley— were into these new ways of connecting with God. The brothers were ministers from a different kind of Christianity but took to the ideas laid out by the Brethren and Pietist groups so much that the brothers talked them up nonstop. Eventually they got a bunch of people to follow their ideas about prayer, fasting, Bible reading, and doing charitable works. This all worked out okay for a while in the Christian circles they were in, but eventually the brothers bugged the leaders at their church so much that they pretty much got the boot. They preached about the personal experience of conversion and the holiness of life, stuff that was individual and not where Christianity was back then.

And that's where Methodism begins. It was one part church tradition, one part personal experience and getting with God by living according to a strict set of principles—a method. That's where the name Methodist comes from. It's this focus on living by a certain rule or method that totally appealed to people when Methodism came to America. Traveling preachers called circuit riders spread Methodist ideas, encouraging people to convert. Nowadays there are a couple of major Methodist groups, with the United Methodist Church (UMC) being just one of them. But there are also a few other kinds of Methodism, two of which are profiled in this section: the African Methodist Episcopal Church and the African Methodist Episcopal Zion Church.

Have I heard of them before?

Almost for sure. The UMC is huge. Seriously, really, really huge. Also, the logo for the church is something pretty catchy. It's a tall cross with a red flame licking up the left side, like it's swirling up to the top or something. The flame is a representation of the Holy Spirit, and you may have seen this logo on a church's sign at some point.

What makes this kind of Christianity unique?

- The Bible is the main deal in Methodism, but the sermons of Methodism's founder, John Wesley, are important too.
- UMC communities are okay with women being ordained as pastors, or bishops.
- UMC churches rely on a prayer book and use the Bible, but modifications and interpretations to these books can be different from church to church, even though everyone's still considered a Methodist Christian.
- Methodists stand by the Social Creed, which is a set of promises to do things like protect God's natural world and the rights of others, to help with poverty, and to support peace and freedom across the globe.

Is there a statement of faith (SOF)?

The Twenty-five Articles of Religion help believers understand and live their faith, and then a few different lists of things are combined into another, bigger book UMC churches use, called *The Book of Discipline*.

Following are some of the main ideas and Bible verses a United Methodist church might focus on:

- Christian fellowship expresses God's love, and the church should welcome everyone unconditionally: 1 Thessalonians 3:12, Mark 9:38–39.
- Living in Christ is the only way to walk as He walked. We're made right by our faith in Him, not by what we can accomplish on our own.
- Between conversion and death is when we grow spiritually and are purified. Being sanctified is an act of God's grace, but you have to work at spiritual perfection: 1 John 5:1, John 3:8.

Who's in charge?

At the top of the UMC is the General Conference. It's the main deal in Methodism where all the beliefs, rules, and other stuff are decided for all UMC communities.

At the local level, a UMC community uses elders and deacons. Elders basically do the stuff that a minister, pastor, or priest does in other kinds of Christian churches, like perform weekly services. Then deacons fill in to do things a church needs to run a complete ministry, like offering music or taking care of the business end of things. But whether you're a higher-up clergy leader or a regular layperson, the UMC has got some of everybody on all their councils and at all their conferences. It's an even-steven kind of thing.

What's the word for people my age?

The UMC has a general online board where lists of events and resources are posted for people in places all across America, and even worldwide: http://www.gbod.org/youth/.

Then you've also got the UMYF (United Methodist Youth Fellowship) website. It's sort of like the general board, but has more of a hang-out feel with chat and forums and what-not: http://umyf.net/.

And last, there's the main UMC youth organization UMYO (United Methodist Youth Organization). The group is cool since it's set up to get young people in touch with older Methodists who run things in a kind of collaboration deal. The UMYO is online at: http://www.umyouth.org/.

Is there anything going on besides church?

Easily one of the coolest things Methodist Christians are doing comes from Methodists in England. They've put together an online church where you log on, pick a little building-block-type girl or guy to be the online version of you, and then choose the service that's led by a building-block-type minister and a whole congregation of other building-block-types who share your interests. Everybody there is from somewhere in the world and is logged on to the Net right then, just like you are. Check out one of their scheduled online services: http://shipoffools.com/church/.

Methodists also have lots of outreach efforts in swing. The main UMC website has a spot called Faith in Action that lists outreach efforts and volunteer opportunities: http://www.umc.org/interior.asp?mid=158.

If you're thinking it'd be great to head to a Christian college, you can do that through the UMC. A magazine called *Orientation* will get you started: http://www.gbhem.org/orientation/home.html. Then visit the website list of Methodist related schools: http://www.umc.org/frames.asp?url=http://www.gbhem.org/gbhem/colleg.html.

How can I hook up with this kind of Christianity?

The main way to find out about UMC Christianity is to visit their main website: http://www.umc.org/index.asp.

For more of a summary on Methodist Christianity in general, look through the website: http://religiousmovements.lib.virginia.edu/nrms/methodist.html.

INDEX